A Lollipop Through

A Lollipop Through the Railings

Enid Farnell

The Pentland Press Limited
Edinburgh • Cambridge • Durham • USA

First published in 1999 by
The Pentland Press Ltd.
1 Hutton Close
South Church
Bishop Auckland
Durham

British Library Cataloguing in Publication Data.
A Catalogue record for this book is available
from the British Library.

ISBN 1 85821 643 5

Typeset by CBS, Martlesham Heath, Ipswich, Suffolk
Printed and bound by Antony Rowe Ltd., Chippenham

This book is dedicated to everyone who has helped in my recovery – you all know who you are.

FOREWORD

So often in life we witness other people's suffering. Daily and graphically on television, we see the pain left behind by floods, fires, hurricanes and other disasters. As survivors are pulled from underneath the rubble, barely holding onto life, we wonder what it was that kept them alive – great courage, determination, true grit? Enid Farnell is a woman who demonstrates all of these, her strength of character tested to the limit after an horrific motorbike crash in which she was dragged under the wheels of a transport tanker. Her injuries were so extensive that doctors thought she wouldn't survive – she lost her left arm and shoulder, most of her collar bone had to be removed, half of her left lung was gone, her sternum was crushed and she had between fifty and sixty breakages in her ribcage. But in the early stages, as now, six years on and still in constant pain, Enid's will to survive has surpassed any physical setbacks. *Lollipop Through The Railings* tells the story of Enid's remarkable courage in her fight for life. With the constant support of her husband Eddie she's achieved more than doctors could ever have imagined. Many of us would feel bitterness at the loss of mobility, having to live with the knowledge that excruciating pain is our lot in life. But Enid's remarkable spirit will allow for none of that – she's thankful for another chance in life and welcomes each day with open arms, no matter what it may have in store. It's a positive attitude Enid attributes to her upbringing in Trimdon Station, a pit village in County Durham. Throughout *Lollipop Through The Railings* Enid looks back to her childhood and, with a language so descriptive it transports you to the village of her youth, tells of the important role her family has played in pulling her through the most difficult of times. *Lollipop Through The Railings* is the tale, told in a moving and often amusing way, of a truly remarkable woman, a real inspiration.

Nicki Chadwick
Journalist and TV Presenter

Chapter 1

A LOLLIPOP THROUGH THE RAILINGS

This is the most uncanny feeling, I must be dreaming. Yes it's a dream, very black and noisy.

It's back again, this time I feel and hear, but I still have no visual images.

The blackness is all around me and I can't seem to rouse myself. I try to feel across the bed for Eddie, but the blackness gets to me once again, so I give up the fight and sleep on till morning.

It is the most persistent dream that I have ever encountered. I can hear strange voices, the darkness seems to fade into a lighter darkness then on into a greyness and I hear Eddie's voice, his lovely gentle voice telling me how much he loves me. Suddenly he asks me a question, 'Do you know where you are, Enid? Do you remember that we had an accident on the bike?'

The bike, yes I remember the bike, the motor cycle that we both love so much, but why do I imagine that I am in Harrogate? I try to reason with myself inside my head, and I decide that not only is this a very strange dream, but that I must also be talking in my sleep again. The soft voice continues, 'You are in Leeds, in the hospital, love.' For some unknown reason Harrogate still seems to loom in my thoughts. The greyness parts and I see my Eddie in front of me. Why does he look so

1

sad? What has happened, and why am I in Leeds? I see a nurse and she appears to speak to me, but I do not hear her words.

I try to concentrate on Eddie's voice as he speaks to me once again, 'Do you want me to tell you what happened, love?' Yes I do, but the words will just not form in my mouth, can I nod? I try to communicate, it's the first time that I can remember being stuck for words! It takes all of my strength and determination, but at last my head moves ever so slightly. Once again the familiar loving voice speaks, "Do you remember the accident?'

Accident, what accident? My mind can't seem to recall anything about an accident.

'Do you want me to tell you about it, love?'

I must have somehow managed to convey to him that I did, because the voice continues. 'We had a road traffic accident, and you were very badly hurt.' I hear his words, but all that I can recall are bright lights and the closeness of something very large and frightening. Eddie's voice continues, 'Do you want me to tell you about your injuries, love?'

Again I somehow manage to gesture to him that I do, and the warm strong voice goes on to tell me that I have lost my left arm. My left arm has been surgically removed. It does not seem to make sense to me, as I can feel the arm, in fact, the pain that I feel is the worst pain that I have ever experienced, but Eddie would never lie to me, and he is crying, my Eddie is crying, please God, let me understand what is happening.

Eddie kisses me and I feel his beard on my face, and I remember the love that we share, a very special relationship. He begins to rise and I see the tears once again, 'Please God, let me touch his face, let me take some of the hurt away from him.' I manage to reach up and touch his face, I feel his face, and I feel his tears, and then I feel no more, the blackness takes over once again.

Chapter 2

FRIGHTENING REALITY

My awareness returned very slowly, I accepted the world of intensive care, and its warmth and constant attention made me feel like a dependent foetus in the womb. It is a feeling that has to be experienced before it can be made into any kind of sense. Each time I opened my eyes, it was to see the face of the man that I loved looking back at me. He had always promised that we would never be parted and that he would never leave me, and I knew that he meant every word. He was then, and will always be my strength.

Time passed very slowly in my world of morphine and countless other lotions and potions. I remember vividly my daughter's beautiful face, my son's lost and worried look, my brother holding my hand, my big brother who has always looked after me, he is a retired miner, and treasures his family as only miners can. Never was I without the feeling that I was loved very much.

Somewhere along the line I realised that the lack of speech on my part was due to the fact that the surgeons had kitted me out with a ventilator. This was more than necessary, for my badly lacerated lungs needed all the help that they could get to provide me with the oxygen to keep me alive. I seemed to have pipes, tubes and drains protruding from every available space which was left on my poor old broken body. I will never cease to marvel at the skill and persistency on the part of the team of surgeons and nursing staff, who had the mammoth task of putting what was left of me back together. I remember the inner panic that I felt, when eventually I had the strength to lift up my right hand to my face. Vanity took over, and besides, I was a little curious too. If I had had the ability to scream, then I think that I might have done so. I appeared to have also been badly disfigured in the crash, my face was covered in scars!

I had to muster up all my strength and courage and, trying not to make Eddie too aware of the panic going on inside of me, I conveyed by gestures and murmurs that I was concerned. I pointed to my face, he seemed to know what I wanted, for he said to me, 'There is nothing wrong with your face, it is just the same as it always was.' I began to cry, so he took my one good hand, and smiling, passed it over my face. He calmly told me that my face was all taped up with micropore, it was there to keep all the tubes in place. The panic abated, what a fool I had been, but to me the scarring felt very real! If I had been my normal self, then I would have remembered that my new crash helmet had full face protection. I hasten to add that the helmet saved my face and head from serious damage.

This episode must have taken place after I had been in hospital for quite some time, but because of the implication of facial disfigurement, my mind seems to have placed it high on the agenda of events. I never had before classed myself as particularly vain, but I now have to admit to the world that I have been found guilty of the sin of vanity! Hopefully one hard lesson that I have learned is that in future it would be more than unwise to make assumptions!

Chapter 3

OUCH!!

I became aware of the extent of my injuries during the first two weeks in hospital. I had been blessed with enough common sense to know that I had been, and probably still was, desperately ill, but the enormity of the situation was not brought home to me until many months after the accident, when the consultant who led the team of surgeons who were responsible for my reconstruction, said to me that to his knowledge, I was the first person to have ever survived the massive crush injuries that I had sustained in the accident. I still shudder, and marvel at how I managed to hold on to life. I like to think that God decided that it wasn't quite my time, and that maybe I was worthy of one more chance. I also knew that I did not want to leave Eddie, and fought desperately, knowing that he was by my side, giving me love, strength and everything else that I needed to survive.

To my despair, during those first two weeks, Eddie told me that I had lost my shoulder along with my left arm, most of my collar bone had to be removed, half of my left lung, and also the ribs to the top left were gone. I had several broken vertebrae in my back, and many more broken in my neck! My sternum was crushed, and I had between fifty and sixty breakages to the remaining ribcage. My left lung had been virtually shredded, hence the need to remove half of it, and my right lung had

Five days before the accident, July 1992 showing shoulder

Two years after the accident, 1994, minus shoulder

been badly punctured by the shattered ribs. Quite an impressive list! My motto at work had always been, 'If you are going to do a job, then make it a good one!' No one could ever accuse me of not doing a good job this time!!

Chapter 4

DEVASTATING EFFECTS

My Mother always taught me that dying was a thing that appeared to get more acceptable as the years went by, but here I was, in my mid forties, and as frightened as ever of the idea of death. I vividly recall during one of my lowest and worst moments saying to God, 'Please let me die, I can't stand any more pain.' It must have been bad, because I have always been horrified of dying, and here I was, praying to be relieved of the precious gift of life. I quickly withdrew the statement, let me add, after much panic, thinking, 'I hope that you are not listening, God, because I really want to live!'

Let me tell you that it would have been so easy to let go on the thread that I had on life, for it appeared to evoke such a warm, comfortable, drifting feeling which held no physical pain or discomfort. After these experiences I now find that I have much less fear of dying. It could be hinted by sceptics that my mind was playing tricks on me, and that I only imagined that I had moved along the pathway to death. Not so! Remember, I have been there, seen it, almost done it, but did not quite like the colour of the tee shirt!

As my mind began to clear and my thoughts once again began to formulate, I started to remember the course of events that led up to the accident. My memory of happenings before the accident was quite clear, but during, and immediately after, appear to have been completely obliterated. It is a strange feeling, not being able to remember the incident that caused my permanent disablement, and these areas of blackness remain with me, even now. Thankfully though, I have been spared from the pain and recollection of falling under the rear triple axle of a fully laden thirty eight ton tanker!

On the day of July 3rd 1992, I got out of bed at six in the morning, had my bath, and then packed the bike panniers for a one night stopover for both Eddie and myself. We planned to take our new bike back to Birmingham, for its first five hundred mile service. Our Triumph 1200 was a wonderful bike, we had only bought it the previous weekend, it was our pride and joy, a culmination of a dream for both of us. Eddie had spent his life around bikes, he loved them, and he taught me to love them too. We planned to spend the whole of our summer vacation touring Scotland, France and anywhere else that took our fancy. This year we had a bonus in the shape of an extra week's holiday, nine instead of the usual eight. We had both followed careers as lecturers in Further Education and this was the last day of the summer term. We were in our mid forties, and would probably have been looked on as 'oldies' by the younger generation of bikers, but to us, age is irrelevant, we had only been together for six months, and we wanted to enjoy each other's company, and be together as much as we possibly could. We planned to marry soon, but we were about to find out that 'the best laid plans of mice and men' were about to be scuppered!

The morning was what we call in the north-east of England drizzly, not heavy rain, but all the same, on a bike it was a real nuisance! Eddie dropped me off at work in Consett, County Durham at about eight in the morning, and then he went back to his college which was in Middlesbrough, Cleveland. He had to sit in on a staff meeting and also attend to the rounding up of the end of year administrative affairs. He telephoned me to say that he would be on his way back to pick me up at lunch time, so I organized coffee and sandwiches.

We had lunch, and we were geared up and on our way by one thirty, heading towards the A1 motorway at Durham City. The weather could by now be classified as somewhat more than the nuisance that it started the day as, and I knew that Eddie was in two minds whether he should turn back or not. As we approached Catterick Garrison the weather had cleared considerably and the rain was only very light. I was thinking how nice that it would be to see Eddie's Mother and Father again, I also knew that there would be a warm welcome, followed closely by a good home cooked meal. Eddie's Mother prides herself in looking after her family, especially Dad, who she still loves with such a strength of feeling that it lifts my spirits to see them together. Even after more than fifty years it is still obvious for all to see, a rare thing in this day and age. I was brought back to reality when the bike slowed down, and we joined the tail end of a very long traffic jam. We trickled along at less that ten miles an hour, which gave me more than enough time to take in the scenery. It was then that I realised that we were adjacent to R.A.F. Dishforth.

The first step in the chain of events that led up to the accident suddenly happened, for a man in a large red car to our left, took the opportunity to clean his misted windows, not a very interesting event on the whole, but it proved to be devastating for us. The driver let his attention wander, and his car drifted towards us, Eddie took evasive action and thankfully we did not exchange any paint. The unfortunate thing was, that in moving out of his way, we ended up in dangerously close proximity, to a very large transport tanker. The next few seconds flashed by.

We apparently hit a patch of mud which had been deposited on the road by a previous driver, and the inevitable happened, the bike just slid from under us. We were doing between five and ten miles an hour at the time. Eddie managed to drag me out from under the tanker, just as it halted, thankfully before the third wheel went over me. The damage done by two wheels of that proportion was indescribable, thank goodness the third wheel missed, or I most definitely would have not survived.

Both Eddie and I have talked long, and shed buckets of tears over the events of the following twenty-four hours. Although Eddie was badly bruised and shaken by the accident, he fortunately went in the opposite direction to me, he instinctively rolled into a ball, whereas I torpedoed at great speed under the enormous back wheels. Eddie tells me that he thought that I had died there and then, and when he found that I was still alive, he prayed that if I was to die there on the road, that God would let me die without pain. I know in my heart what torment he must have been going through, but I also thank God that the situation had not been reversed, as Eddie had extensive experience with the St John's Ambulance Brigade, and he automatically knew what to do. I shudder to think just what might have happened if I had been in his place, and he in mine, because of my ignorance of the subject, I would not have been able to do anything other than watch him die.

Eddie kept me alive until the ambulance arrived, he was able to give them vital information, such as the fact that he had seen the neck being broken, and that both lungs were badly lacerated. Something else that, although it was not outwardly evident, was an important factor, the fact that I was, and still am horribly claustrophobic, and can't bear my face covered.

Chapter 5

DRIPS, DRAINS AND CATHETERS!

The nearest hospital to the scene of the accident was Harrogate General. I must have been quite a rare case, as the enormity of my injuries could not be coped with at such a small hospital. They did however provide a very vital link in the chain for they managed to establish an airway, and they took the decision to try and get me to St James Hospital in Leeds. It was thought that with their track record, they just might have the expertise to save my life. So I was deposited in the ambulance, along with a team of three doctors and two nurses, and with a police escort they went at breakneck speed to 'Jimmies,' providing me with what they felt was my best chance of survival.

The following hours must have been awful for Eddie, for the prognosis was made at Jimmies that I might not live long enough for them to operate. He sat through lengthy discussions with the team of surgeons, they needed to know every detail of why, how, where and when the accident took place. He assumed that their thoroughness enabled them to assess the situation, and decide upon a plan of action. Apparently I was squashed completely flat on my left side, and the jigsaw that was presented to them, had either to be pieced back together, or surgically removed.

Throughout the night, time after time the operation was

scheduled, but one crisis after another in my condition, delayed it. The situation was looking very bleak when finally the next morning, Frank, one of the team, said to Eddie, 'If we don't do it now, then we will never do it.' He followed this stark statement with, 'Chances are she won't make it through the surgery.' I have said these words over and over to myself, and I have tried desperately to visualise the scene, but try as I may, I do not seem to be able to convince myself, that it was me that this terrible thing was happening to. Maybe it's my brain's way of not accepting the loss of the limb, I do not know, but I hope the realisation does not hit me one day, or then I might feel like I have once again been knocked down by the thirty-eight tonner!

The worst possible scenario followed, the damage was so vast and life threatening, that all the team could do was to remove everything that would contra-indicate the saving of my life, which was by then, hanging by the slenderest of threads.

Mr Batchelor the plastic surgeon who led the team, came to see me in the H.D. Unit when I was coherent enough to understand what he was saying. He looked at me sadly and said, 'I'm so sorry that we could not save more, but I promise you that by doing what we did, we increased your chances of survival.' I knew that the surgeons at Jimmies were world famous for their pioneering work, and I also knew that they must have felt a slight pang of remorse that in my case they had failed to save the arm. I will remember my reply forever: 'Think nothing of it, I'm alive and life is sweet, I will learn to live without the arm.' This might sound blasé to some people, but I assure you that it was not my intention to be so, and I believe in my heart of hearts, that this was the very moment in time, that I began to believe that survival was possible, and that if I tried hard enough, then I just might be able to pull it off.

Chapter 6

FORGOTTEN JOURNEY

Time was endless during our stay in the hospital, the nights felt about three times longer than I had remembered them to be, the days seemed to drag by at a snail's pace, and the final insult came with the realisation that they served an awful cup of tea! Eddie put up with it all and had the patience of Job. I was later told that when the surgeons had asked him what he wanted to do during my stay in hospital, he replied, 'I intend to stay here with Enid, and when she is well enough to go home, then we will go home together.' He is a remarkable man, and I love him dearly. Thankfully the hospital was sympathetic to his wishes. They very wisely realised that the healing process for both of us, must include the fact that we needed to be together, so they very kindly furnished Eddie with a small room for the duration of our stay. It was a gesture that we will both always be eternally grateful for. During the early days in Jimmies, the job of contacting family and friends fell to Eddie, he did an admirable job under the circumstances, especially when it was to be remembered that he was far from being in A1 condition himself.

My first days of awareness were spent in an atmosphere of extreme sickness, and unmerciful pain. It was at this time that I became aware that I had been introduced to an invaluable and life saving piece of equipment during the operation. I mentioned before that I required the aid of a ventilator to keep me breathing, what I didn't mention was the fact that I was terrified of the contraption! I think that I will carry the fear of the thing forever. I must sound like an ungrateful wretch, but anyone who has ever experienced the fear that wells up inside when the nurse has to manually clear the airway when the poor patient has just been sick, will know exactly what I mean. I suppose in my case the fact that I am claustrophobic only aggravated the situation. To be totally helpless, lying prone on the back, with no means of moving or the ability to help oneself, choking and suffocating both at the same time, is an experience that I would never wish to repeat. I used to visibly shake every time the nurse came near me with the tube. I even at one time convinced myself that one of the nurses got a sense of enjoyment out of the act. Eddie told me later that she was an exceptionally good nurse, very efficient, but he felt that her one failing was that she always appeared to be unsympathetic to my personal anxiety. I pray that she forgives me for my suspicions, but I know that she will understand that I was not quite my level headed self at the time!

I do not seem to remember the journey that I made from the Intensive Care Unit through to the High Dependency Unit, I must have been under the influence of morphine, or just simply unconscious, because I was moved, lock stock and barrel, up one floor, via the lift! My stay in H.D.U. again was a time of extreme pain, but with a growing awareness of my new surroundings and recently acquired circumstances. There are many special relationships, formed in this unique environment, and it is ironic that it was at this time that my memory appeared to begin to re-store everyday information, and therefore the recent hazy memories of the I.C.U. pale somewhat.

This does not deny the fact that without the expert care and attention that the staff of the I.C.U. lavished on me, then I would not have been made well enough to be subsequently moved on to the next stage of recovery.

During this time in H.D.U. I began unconsciously to formulate what was to be part of my plan of campaign to recovery. I was not aware at the time what I was actually doing, but in retrospect I appeared to be planning my day to day progress towards recovery. I set out my goals to aim for. I remember desperately wanting to be strong enough to be able to begin to breathe for myself. Hopefully this would see the demise of the dreaded ventilator. I awoke each morning with the hope that one more tube, drain or drip might meet its end! Very slowly, oh so very slowly, one by one my wishes came true. Out came the dreaded ventilator and along with it went my voice, my throat was so sore that I could only whisper, but nevertheless, I felt that progress was being made, my lungs were healing at last!

H.D.U. was a very small and specialised unit, it contained only four beds. The nurses were a marvel, they kept constant vigil from their workstation, both by day and by night. It is a situation where one nurse has responsibility for just two patients, but on occasion when the unit is not fully occupied then it was reduced to a one to one situation. At the time of my residency there were only three of us in there. My two companions were, Margaret, a lady who was recovering from brain surgery, and Andrew, a young man, who like ourselves, had been involved in a motor cycle accident. He had been unlucky enough to have come in contact with a car driver who had fallen asleep at the wheel, the man had careered across the central reserve and taken out Andrew and his girlfriend, Jenny. Andrew was badly smashed up, but luckily he was in a repairable state, poor Jenny was less fortunate, she lost her leg, she was only twenty-one at the time.

Chapter 7

TROPICAL CLIMATE

Eddie and Andrew often talked together about bikes, and I was happy that he had found a kindred spirit. I was totally surrounded by love, Eddie had brought my favourite things for me, a photograph that we had taken on a recent trip to Cragside, in Northumberland, where we had such a good day – just looking at it evoked such wonderful memories. By my bedside was Spiker, my favourite toy hedgehog, Eddie had bought him for me on our first weekend in the Dales. Our favourite music played very softly in the background, and for us both, the most important things were the photographs of our children and grandchildren.

Our daily routine usually began at six thirty each morning. I was so helpless and weak that I had to be bed bathed with as little disturbance as was possible. I might add that Eddie would have passed muster with Miss Nightingale herself! I was washed and carefully dried, and liberally dusted over with talcum powder in ever conceivable crack and crevice. I'm sure that Eddie has seen parts of me that I never even knew existed. He then changed my sheets, and ever so carefully repositioned me and my pillows on the special bed that I appeared to be floating on; it was hooked up to a compressor, and the constant stream of moving air passing through it was meant to alleviate bed sores and make me as comfortable as was possible. Over all Eddie was magnificent, he tended to all my needs, and I knew that it was all done with much love and care.

One of the main causes of discomfort whilst in H.D.U. was the very high temperature at which it was kept, eighty-four degrees, or thereabouts!

Bearing in mind that my mattress was completely encased in plastic, you can imagine I did not need to subscribe to a health club for I had my own personal sauna right there! I lay there and melted, and I must have been the bane of Eddie's life for I have always had a life long love affair with personal hygiene and had a horror of becoming sweaty and smelly! I must have been the most bed bathed patient in Jimmies. I shouldn't jest, because there was a very good reason for maintaining such tropical temperatures, for the majority of patients in the unit had been involved in some form of plastic surgery or other, and skin grafting necessitates such measures.

Pain was a constant bedfellow and still causes me the greatest concern to this day, but the huge amount of physical pain, combined with the relentless nerve pain, seemed to completely overwhelm me at times. This was the time that I was introduced to a contraption that appeared to give me morphine on demand. Sounds like a junkie's paradise, but never fear, it was set to give only a specific amount, in a prescribed time span. It was taped to my hand, and it provided me with several small shots each hour, thus giving me my first feeling that I had some control over my own pain relief. The morphine entered my body by means of an arterial spur, which had previously been inserted into the right side of my neck. At first I had great difficulty just holding the contraption, let alone making contact with the control button. Let me tell you that when I realised its great benefits, then it was amazing how quickly I learned to use it. It was astounding how adept I became with this technique, the

18

nurse would always give me plenty of warning if examinations or X-rays were to be carried out where it would necessitate me being moved, and a few minutes beforehand I would give myself a shot of morphine. It was not a completely pain free procedure, but it certainly helped, mentally as well as physically.

Chapter 8

MY MAM

My Mam was constantly in my thoughts, she had been thirty-eight when I was born, and to her I would always be 'her baby'. She had reached the age of eighty-two, and because of arthritis and acute sciatica, she was having great difficulty when walking, in fact on occasion she had to resort to using a wheelchair. She had recently bought herself what she jokingly called 'her bike'. This was a walking frame which was equipped with wheels, and also handbrakes. It gave her a little more independence, which she valued very highly. Throughout her life she had always been a very hard working lady, because of this, I grew up in two home environments, my parents' home, and the home of my gentle Aunty Mary, she was my Mam's older sister, and she possessed a very quiet nature. In my infancy my Mam worked as a ward cleaner at Sedgefield General Hospital. In those days a ward cleaner's duties covered a multitude of skills, much different from the modern day equivalent, it was very hard physical work, with little or no electrical equipment, so the term 'elbow grease' really did apply. The regime was very strict and orderly and the Matron saw to it that it remained firmly in her control. In those days it was she who ran the hospital, not the management team. Even in such a Labour stronghold, for Mannie Shinwell was the M.P. at the time, women were very poorly paid, and expected not to complain about it, the days of women's lib and equality were still many years hence.

My dominant childhood memories include an abundance of house moves, sixteen in all, and all within the confines of the same small pit village. My Mam was quite a business woman, and she bought and sold small houses and shops at an alarming rate.

My Dad always maintained that when he came home from work in the evening, he was never quite sure if he had to return to the same house that he had left that morning! The love of my Mam's life always was her fish and chip shops, and the older inhabitants of Deaf Hill still remember her prowess at frying what was to many, the best fish and chips in County Durham. The frying was done on a range, heated by coal fires, and involved the use of the best beef dripping, a process that would be much frowned upon by today's healthy society, but I still remember the taste, rarely have I tasted their equal, never have I tasted better, and after all these years my mouth still waters at their delicious memory. Her own health had been quite robust until she was about seventy-eight, then the formative years of hard work took their toll. Although in constant pain, she insisted on living by herself in her little bungalow, and thankfully she kept her fierce independence until she died, which sadly she did, on October 5 1992. No one will ever be able to convince me that the shock of my accident did not play a great part in her death.

My brother Matty had thought that it was wise that until I looked in a more recognisable state, he should try to make excuses for not bringing her on the long journey to see me. I agreed with him, but I knew that she would be going through the same emotional turmoil as I was. He must have had his work cut out for him, as I knew that my Mam could be very strong, and unbelievably determined when she felt that it was necessary. We did speak on the telephone, and it made me feel a little easier when I heard her voice; she told me that she loved me, and that she thought I was the bravest person in the world; she went on to say that she was so glad that I had found someone like Eddie, to love and care for me. In the face of all this pain and upset, she still thought that I was a very lucky lady. Looking back on this conversation, I am convinced that she was in some way trying to tell me that she knew that her time on earth was limited, that she would have peace of mind about my future, and it would be easier for her to go when she was called on, to the next world to be with my Dad.

Chapter 9

ADDY UPS AND TAKE-AWAYS!

One of my first visitors whilst in H.D.U. was the principal of
the college where I had worked for the past six years. I was still
very groggy at the time, but I have a vivid recollection of Judith
Round and her secretary Jean Jackson standing by my bed. They
had travelled all the way from Consett in County Durham just
to see me, bringing with them a letter from the college Board
of Governors, wishing me well, and assuring me that I still had
a job to go back to when I was fully recovered. Work had for
many years played a very important part in my life, and when I
was well enough to read the letter for myself, I was pleased to
think that I still figured in the plans within the college
environment. Eddie had a chat to them both whilst I was drifting
in and out of consciousness, and he said how impressed he was
with their genuine concern, and the fact that they had travelled
so far for such a short visit. The world is a better place because
of such genuine friends. The get well cards and flowers began
to roll in, and we decided to keep a count of them. I felt that it
might help to improve my powers of concentration if I did a
few simple calculations, my poor old brain felt that it was totally
under the influence of morphine, and this seemed as good a
time as any to get the old grey matter working again. I did not
like the side affects that the drugs had on me, I felt continually

drunk, my tongue felt swollen and thick, my mouth was excessively dry, and the final insult was that I was having difficulty forming certain words. My memory had taken quite a battering, and the continued use of such strong pain killers did not help. On occasion I even thought that for kindness' sake the doctors were not telling me all of the facts, and maybe my poor brain would remain so befuddled forever. Thank goodness I was wrong! By the time I was ready to leave the hospital, I was able to see a vast improvement in my own functioning, and totalled up the number of cards to one hundred and six.

Our children were never far from our thoughts, the eldest Sara, was twenty-four, married to Neil, and then had two children, Matthew four, and Faine just six months old. She has since had another baby girl, who she named after my Mam, Jennie, my Mother would have been so proud of the tribute paid to her. David was twenty, and an apprentice bricklayer, Melanie fifteen, and preparing for her final year at school, and last but not least, Lucie thirteen, who can only be described as a loving and giving child. Sara and David had seen me at my very worst, and hopefully because of their age, were better able to cope with the trauma of it all, not knowing for so long whether I would live or die. They never once in those frightening early days, made me feel that I appeared any different than I had before the accident, which for me was a great morale booster, because I still had not been given the courage to look at myself in the mirror. I gained strength in the knowledge that they truly believed that I was going to survive, God bless them. Melanie and Lucie were allowed in after a few days, I knew that I needed to see them, and also to see how they had coped with it all. They were marvellous, it was so good to see them, I knew that Lulu was desperate to cry but they both managed to hide their emotions admirably, only the hurt in their eyes gave them away.

I guessed that after the visit was over, they must have just made it to the corridor before they gave vent. We love all four of them, and pray that their lives be filled with as much love and happiness as they have brought to Eddie and me.

Slowly but surely, as the days progressed, out came all the paraphernalia of needles, drips, and drains, until all that I was left with was a hosepipe of a chest drain, which entered by means of a huge man made gash in my chest, it then led all the way into the pleural cavity, and was externally attached to a vacuum suction pump, which kept the chest cavity clear of excess fluids, it reminded me of something that I had seen on Doctor Who. The second contraption that I was still firmly fixed to was a great source of embarrassment to me, for I had been catheterised, the bag being so strategically placed as to allow my visitors a good look at its contents! I did not know which one I disliked the most, the pain of the chest drain, or the indignity of all and sundry being able to see me pass water!

The remainder of my body was what my Mam would have called 'variegated', it seemed to go from black to blue, purple to yellow, and in some areas it could have even been classified as green, there did not appear to be many areas that still had a respectable pink hue! I could not have been termed as anything other than looking like an explosion in a paint factory. I was also considerably thinner, something that I had spent the best part of my adult life yearning to be, slim and sylph like! Let me tell you though, this method of weight reduction is not to be recommended, it is much less painful to join a slimming group, and only be parted with your cash! Eddie was also much slimmer, he devoted so much of his time to my needs that I never seemed to remember him taking time out to eat, but I did know that he was not silly enough to neglect the needs and requirements of his stomach. I also knew that trauma and stress could be a desperate thing to bear. Up until this moment I had not been able to contribute any of my time to his welfare, and so I decided that now might be the time for me to try and involve myself again and begin to talk of our future plans together, also for our wedding, and as many of our long term and positive commitments as we possibly could. I loved him dearly and I needed him to know that I would not let anything change our future life together. I was at this time just about well enough to be transferred to a private room on the plastics ward. The day had been particularly arduous where pain was concerned, so they decided to give me a massive dose of morphine, in the hopes that the transfer of surroundings could take place with as little discomfort as possible to myself, and also to allow both Eddie and I to get a little sleep and much needed rest. The night staff nurse in charge of the new ward instructed Eddie not to return until noon the following day. The decision worried him, but he was wise enough to accept the ruling gracefully as he did not want to tread on anyone's toes. Off he went to his little room to try and sleep.

I awoke in the early hours in a complete panic! I had reacted very badly to the morphine and could not remember the circumstances of the move into the new room, and so the surroundings were completely alien to me. It was dark and I was very frightened and appeared to be concerned about the dimensions of the room, and what exactly was to the rear of my bed. I could hear strange noises, which I later learned were the heating systems, the lift shaft and the helicopter landing area, the noises in the dark were terrifying.

The worst thing that I had to cope with was the fact that Eddie was not there! Luckily just then the night staff did their rounds and they showed me how to summon help if I needed it. The poor nurses were so busy that night that they probably didn't have time to read my notes and realise that until that moment I had never been able to cope with any physical tasks; I had had the benefit of Eddie's constant care, and I suppose they did not have the time that night to stop and think of the possible consequences. The button to summon assistance was situated on the side of the locker to the right of my head, but because of my neck and spinal injuries, I couldn't even reach out with my one good arm to press for assistance. I was alone for quite some time, and to all intents and purposes, my brain seemed to think that I was in a room in the basement, try as I could I hadn't the wherewithal to convince myself otherwise. I suppose the drugs plus the sheer panic, made for devastating results. After what seemed like a lifetime the night nurse returned and I asked if there was any other way of attracting their attention. She was very nice, and arranged for a small table to be placed near my right hand, and she placed on it a small brass bell which was the means of summoning help, but after she had left the room, I found that the practicality of the action still eluded me, for I still did not have the strength or the co-ordination to pick up the bell. I suddenly felt overwhelmingly and totally lost, unbelievably alone, and so terribly inadequate, in this unknown and dark environment, my claustrophobia switched into overdrive, my mind worked overtime, and the realisation dawned on me just how terrifyingly inadequate and vulnerable I was when it came to helping myself. Never again would I be able to hold Eddie when we kissed, never again would I feel safe enough to hold my baby grand-daughter, never again would I be able to teach all the specialist practically based skills that I loved so much. I have always been a tactile creature, and love, and the showing of affection, comes high on my list of priorities, and so suddenly the magnitude of my loss totally overwhelmed me. I was lost in a sea of self pity, and I did not like the feeling one bit. The loss to me felt like a bereavement, so much heartache, so much pain, and so very final and irreversible. I cannot portray to you the intensity of terror and hopelessness that took over my whole body and mind, the one person that could help me was Eddie, and I knew that he was not going to be there for hours. Night slowly progressed into day, and still the terror remained. The night staff were changing shifts with the day staff, and when the young staff nurse came in to introduce herself she very quickly picked up on my obvious distress. I found that she had a very good listening ear, and I was relieved that she did not appear to think that I was as weak willed as I thought that I was, for by now, I had a very low opinion of myself. She sat and held my hand, listening compassionately to me amid the tears, I told her of my special relationship with Eddie, how we needed to be together, and how this need appeared to play a major part in our personal healing process. Eddie and I are so close that we often think the same thoughts, and regularly speak the same words at the same time. She hung onto my hand and said that it was her belief that the psychological effect created by the sudden move of surroundings, and the subsequent loss of Eddie's support, even if it was only for a limited period, could be more than detrimental to me in my acceptance of the loss of the limb. She very kindly pleaded my case to the day ward sister who thankfully agreed with her, she then phoned through to Eddie's room, he apparently was up and dressed, and as agitated as I was. He had been trying to occupy his mind, and pass the time until noon came around. He ran the mile and a half through the corridors to be with me.

When I saw his face in the doorway of my room, the terror started to leave me, and the relief must have been plain for all to see. A long time has elapsed since, but I still need his strength to help me through each day, and our love gets deeper and stronger with the passing of time.

Chapter 10

PATIENCE IS A VIRTUE

I was unfortunate enough not to have had any sisters of my own, but I will always class my sister-in-law, Edna, and my friend, Lynne McBean, as the next best thing. Lynne and I have been close for many years, she has always been a great source of support for me. She was one of my most constant visitors, and she brought me lots of feminine things, she even bought me some body creams and a battery operated vibro massage machine, to try to get me interested in once again taking care with my appearance, instilling in me the need to feel attractive again. She is a very genuine person and I can always count on her for an honest opinion, whether it is what I really want to hear or not, I know that she would never fob me off just for the sake of it. We used to work together as part of the same Y.T.S. co-ordinating team in F.E. in Middlesbrough, Cleveland, in fact she was my immediate superior. I have her to thank for many things, one of the most important being the fact that she taught me to have confidence in my own abilities, the outcome being that I was then able to use this new found confidence to go on to apply for a higher teaching post, running a brand new section, in another county, and for a totally new authority. She is a true friend and a remarkable person, and when she reads this testimony to her, she will accuse me of senility!!!

Our family and friends were allowed in to visit us in droves, I'm sure that we must have broken every rule in the book! I can honestly say that every day was filled with the joy that can only come from the knowledge that so many of my family and friends, whom I cared for very much, obviously cared for me also. They all played such an important part in my recovery, that I know that it would be impossible to repay their love and kindness.

In the third week of my hospitalisation, I finally got to see my Mam, my brother could not in all honesty find any more plausible excuses, he must have by this time been worn to a frazzle, as she was very astute and probably knew all along what was going on.

Eddie helped me with my preparations and together we tried to make my hair look less like it had not seen soap and water for three weeks. We must have managed some semblance of normality, because I will never forget the look on her face when she was wheeled into my room. The look of relief was difficult for her to hide, I suppose that she had suspected the very worst, but luckily I must have appeared presentable. I kept the covers well over my non-existent left side – one step at a time. Thankfully she accepted that this probably was the right time for her to come and see me. She didn't quibble, she just positioned her wheelchair so as to be close enough to enable her to hold my hand, and I was sure that she was in control again, when she started telling everyone what to do. Out of the shopping bag came all manner and means of goodies, fresh fruit, chocolates, biscuits, and the love of my young life, a big bag of homemade toffee, but these things were only the material things, and were not as important as the real reason for the visit, which was of course to see if I was being looked after to her standards. The parental advice far outweighed any other issue, she was reassured that the hospital was doing its job correctly, both Eddie and I were told just what to do, and more important, what not to do! When she had dotted all the Is and crossed all the Ts, she then announced to my brother that she was happy enough to return to her village and await my release from hospital. She wept a little, and smiled a lot, and so I felt much easier about the situation. My brother then wheeled her off along the corridor to begin the long journey back to Durham. I might add that the indignation that she once held for the wheelchair, seemed to meet its end, when she saw the great potential of being wheeled around places like the Metro Shopping Centre in Gateshead, she forever after made a formidable opponent in the wheelchair stakes, she was more like a formula one racing driver when in charge of that chair, and not the least like someone's sweet old Granny!!

True characters like my Mam are a rare breed nowadays, their passing, I believe, will not only be a sad affair for all who have known them, but in such a small community such as a pit village, it will be highly unlikely that future generations will ever see their like again.

I looked at my room after my Mam had left, it made me very happy to be surrounded by all the beautiful flower arrangements, and baskets of fruit, I imagined the plight of some of the patients in the main wards, who never seemed to have any visitors, and I felt very fortunate, and an extremely lucky lady to be surrounded by the evidence of everyone's affection. I did some more of my daily calculations, the brain wasn't quite up to Mensa standards yet, but I managed to achieve a total of twenty-six baskets of flowers, six bouquets and four large baskets of fruit, and last but not least, a box of the most exquisite, hand made Belgian chocolates. It was just my luck that my appetite was at its worst at this time, and my weight had hit an all time low, so as you can imagine, it grieved me not to be able to get stuck into all these naughties, I hasten to add that there did not appear to be anything wrong with Eddie's appetite, all that worry on my part about him losing weight, thankfully had been for nothing, for when I appeared to show an improvement in my health, then amazingly, his appetite appeared also to go from strength to strength!

I used to lie there on my special bed amid the flowers and dream of being able to languish in a big bath full of warm soapy water, I would have done almost anything to laze in warm soapy water infused with gallons of bubble bath! It was such a great desire, that it became my next goal, so every day during the doctor's rounds I would beg them to sanction the bath. I did realise that the delay in allowing the request was mainly due to the fact that I was still attached to the main chest drain, not forgetting the delightful catheter! They both nestled in their respective habitats, awaiting their liberation. So to coin a phrase, I had to be a patient patient, still they say everything comes to he who waits, and finally the doctor told me that I would see the demise of the dreaded catheter, at some point during that day. I must have acquired a warped sense of humour because it still amuses me to think of the events that led up to the removal. I waited all day for the great moment, evening came, and after my ten o'clock medication Eddie stayed with me until I fell asleep, then he retired to his bed also, we both assumed that the task had been postponed for one more day. At three in the morning, I was aroused by the night staff, with the news that they had arrived to carry out the extraction! I inquired as to the reasoning behind the job being carried out in the middle of the night. The nurse very kindly explained, that the day sister had left several duties to be carried out by the night staff, and apparently I was one of these duties. I had been catheterised once before, after I had had my hysterectomy, and so I had an inclination as to what might follow, as history often repeats itself. It proved to be a painless extraction, and I heaved a sigh of relief at the thoughts of actually having a pee through the normal channels. I certainly got my wish, for every thirty minutes or so throughout the remainder of the night, I required the urgent services of a bedpan. I'm not sure who was the most worn out, me or the nurses, my bladder certainly picked a fine time to assert itself!!

The final hurdle in the Bath Stakes, came a few days later, when the doctors decided to remove the chest drain. It proved to be a mite more awkward than expected, it had been sewn into position whilst I was unconscious, and so I had no idea as to what lurked beneath the surface, I only knew that it had caused me many sleepless nights, because of the discomfort it created. I could hardly believe my eyes when it was taken out, for I did not imagine that my chest was harbouring a tube of such length and diameter, no wonder it was painful! The hole that remained needed to be drawn up into a purse string suture, and it looked and felt like the gathered up neck of my old school duffle bag! I had assumed that the pain would disappear as soon as the drain was removed, but I was proven wrong, for it still is extremely sensitive to touch or to pressure of any kind.

The lung now had to learn to fend for itself, and it also had to learn to deal with the excess fluids. Although the left lung was greatly reduced in size, it appeared to be coping, I smiled to myself and thought, 'Just goes to show what a tough old boot I really am!!'

Chapter 11

LOADS OF BUBBLES, AND SELF PITY

My immediate objective was to have that bath! I felt just a little antisocial by now, even with the loving attention, and constant bed baths that I received from Eddie, I still yearned for the joys and delights of a hot bath, but I found that I was required to prove to the staff nurse that I could support myself long enough, so as not to be at risk whilst in the water. I was more than grateful for Eddie's physical strength, as I needed to be lifted from my lying down position, to a sitting up position, and then forcibly kept there! Even with my much diminished body weight, I found that there was little that I could do to help myself. It for all the world felt like I was sitting in a bowl of jelly, with a spine made from rubber! My ultimate goal was to stand, and eventually walk a few steps, as this I was told was the key to escape and home, however the problem to hand was more than enough for the time being. I have long since struggled with the problem of raising myself from a lying, to a sitting position, and I have come to the conclusion that this objective is either out of my reach in my present condition, or hopefully just a long way from achievement. Still I thank God for the mobility that I do possess.

With lots of practice, and buckets of blood, sweat and tears, and I have to admit, one or two moments of swearing and frustration, we made it to the bathroom. No matter how many expertly administered bed baths I had, let me tell you that there is no substitute for the reality of soaking in the glories of a tub of hot soapy water!

My very neglected hair showed a vast improvement when it was treated to a good scrub, it had been sorely neglected since the accident, I had always been used to a daily shampoo and blow dry routine, and here I was, carrying three weeks' muck about on my hair! I shudder to think of it now, but I must have looked a treat, my crowning glory, strongly resembled the roof of an old thatched cottage. Still, I both looked, and felt like a different person after the ablutions, and to me it was one more step along the road of achievement. Bouts of self pity began to hit me at regular intervals, and as ever Eddie seemed to know just what to do to stop the self destruction, he always managed to solve each newly arisen problem. I believe that I experienced my second worst moment when I realised that I could no longer take for granted my ability to carry out my own day to day living routine. My mind raced from one negative thought to the next negative thought. It grieved me greatly that I could no longer hold my mirror and apply my make-up, my ego took another blow when the realisation struck home that I would never be able to knit for my daughter's children, or do the intricate crochet work that gave me so much pleasure and afforded me great relaxation. I could no longer decorate, or cook family meals, tie my own shoe laces, worse still how was I going to fasten my bra and stockings? I began to slide down the slippery slope of despair into what seemed to be a bottomless pit. My self pity was brought to an abrupt halt, and Eddie brought me back to reality, he said that if I did not try to adopt a more positive way of thinking, then I would prolong my stay in hospital, and I'd never achieve my ambition to go home.

I suppose that the list of minuses could have been endless if

I had been allowed to carry on and fully explore the possibilities, but once again Eddie came to my rescue and made me think of the positive things that I could still do unaided: I could dress my hair, write, read, feed myself, help wash myself, and as he pointed out, there definitely wasn't anything wrong with my ability to communicate. All of these things and many more could be improved upon in the fullness of time, I would have to be a little less than a perfectionist, and accept help gracefully. So I began to climb back out of the pit of self pity, and once again prepared myself to tackle the next obstacle that would surely come hurtling my way.

I still do on occasion grieve for my poor old left arm, I took it for granted for over forty years, but I still believe that I am luckier than some, for there are people in this world who are unfortunate enough to be born without any arms, so I'll learn to adapt and hopefully the self pity will fade.

Chapter 12

BEST TAKEN IN SMALL DOSES!

The next challenge came hurtling at me, at what appeared to be an alarming speed – Eddie convinced me that I had been putting off the day of the great unveiling for far too long, he convinced me that now was the time to take a look at the new, customised version of myself. Luckily for me, I only had with me at the time of the accident a small powder compact, and so I knew that I could just survey one small area at a time, and as this had to be done from a prone position the result appeared deceptively less severe. I did not get a full view of myself until I eventually left hospital. The sight that peered back at me from that small mirror was somehow unreal, I looked like a mannequin in a department store window before the window dresser had finished putting the arm back, only my image was much more exaggerated, for my shoulder was also missing. My brain must have been in total confusion, or maybe it was in denial syndrome, because I distinctly remember thinking, 'From now on, I'm going to permanently have an off the shoulder look!' Daft, I know, but that's what sprang to my befuddled mind. I then caught sight of my puncture wounds, they certainly made me look like a refugee from the St Valentine's Day Massacre!! Over all I decided to take experience of viewing the new me, slowly, and in very small doses. It would take some getting used to.

The next day when the doctors did their ward rounds they cautiously mentioned at a relevant point in the conversation, the word 'Prosthesis.' They explained that the shoulder could be replaced with a custom made job, and that they could even make me a substitute arm. I then inquired of them if the arm would be functional, or would it just hang there? The answer was as I had expected, in no way could it ever be functional, I had lost too much for it to be anything other than cosmetic. As you can imagine this was not what I wanted to hear, I desperately wanted someone to say, 'Yes, we will give you a replacement that is not only functional, but will look realistic too.' I knew what I must do, and suddenly a calmness replaced the disappointment, and I said to them, 'Well, you can keep your arm, it will be of no use to me, it will only get caught in drawers, and car doors and the like, but I will take you up on the offer of a new shoulder.'

The doctors said that they were glad that I had such a positive attitude about the whole thing, but at the time I felt that I was being honest, rather than positive, and I suppose that somewhere along the line, honesty and positive thinking must be linked up. Anyway, who was I to disagree with the experts!

They also said that my positive attitude would go a long way in the acceptance of the loss of the arm, at the time I thought that I had already accepted it. Remember the promise that I made about assumptions? Well, I have learned since that the brain is a very complex creature, and I know that only when the brain relieves me of the devastating effects of phantom limb pain will I be able to begin to accept that it has really gone!

Phantom limb pain, whoever gave it such a silly name obviously never suffered from the condition themselves, if they had, then they would have called it something other than 'Phantom', because that's just what it is not!!

I will try to explain how the pain's existence was justified to me by the pain specialist. Due to the extremely severe damage caused to my central nervous system during the accident my nerve endings, or rather what was left of them, were in a state known as 'confusion', and unfortunately, in my case, not only were the nerves irreparably damaged, but the little sockets that they pass through on entering the spine had also been lost, this made it impossible for the surgeons to relocate any of the damaged nerves. The brain has ever since been constantly receiving confused messages from the nerve endings, and so it still regards the arm as existing. The brain responds to the confusion and remembers the last coherent message that it received from the arm, and unfortunately for me, that seems to have been during the accident. So this is the pain it sends back. If this does not get the desired response, then the brain will send out more pain of a greater intensity. It is an endless cycle of pain, a Catch 22 situation. It appears to have three distinct levels of severity, and it has the ability to make me fully aware of the amputated left hand and arm, one hundred per cent of the time. I know that the arm is gone, but because the brain won't accept the fact then I am made aware of their existence, and actually feel them.

Level one of my pain never switches off, only if I eventually manage to sleep do I get a modicum of respite, although it is not sleep as you would experience it, for I sleep with the awareness of the arm's existence in a badly damaged state, so sleep for me can never be classed as deep sleep, instead, it tends to be superficial. It has the annoying ability to wake me at any given time during the night, by sending out sharp bursts of pain at regular intervals. I marvel that the brain never appears to get tired of these antics, for I know that I certainly do! Anyone reading the following account of phantom limb pain, will, I'm sure, find it very difficult to comprehend, and the fact that all three levels of pain manifest themselves in an arm and hand, that was thrown into a hospital incinerator on July 4th. 1992.

I have my own interpretation of level one pain, I feel that it has similarities to severe circulatory disorders that I have read about. The hand appears to be very swollen and cold, and non-responsive, a bit like frostbite I suppose, the pain is centred in the ends of the fingers, the knuckles and the joints. The skin seems to be swollen to almost bursting point, and the thumb and the fingernails, on occasion, feel as if they are tearing into the flesh of the hand. I have no control over the movement of the limb, but it has on occasion, been known to emulate the movement of the right limb, this strange phenomenon gets less apparent as time passes, unfortunately the pain does not.

Level two pain is an extension of level one pain; it's as if they join forces, so to speak. The fingers appear to be forced into the most unnatural positions, I have often felt that objects the size of golf balls are being forced in between the digits, and the pressure exerted is tremendous and very fierce, as is the pain.

Levels one and two then join forces with their 'big sister', to create level three. When I experience pain at this intensity, I find it very hard to maintain any control at all, it is something akin to being plugged into the national grid. Without any warning, at a rate of frightening regularity, some unseen hand keeps throwing the switch on, and then slowly back off again. With this level I find that I cannot control my muscles, and I shake violently in the few seconds between jolts, and as one spasm tapers away, I have little or no time to prepare myself for the next. The pain is obviously nerve centred, the nearest description that I can offer is that it feels like many guitar strings that are being plucked together; there is no sound, but the pain reverberations build up as the string is lifted higher, they all reach a vicious crescendo, then when it is finally released the reverberations get less, and the pain eases slightly. It can on my worst days, peak and trough like this for hours on end, I have no indication as to what causes the onslaught, nor do I know what to do to make it abate. The side effects of a bad day are many and varied, I usually vomit, have violent headaches, develop pulled stomach muscles but the most disconcerting of them all is the bruising that can take place. I have on many occasions been left with severe bruising around my neck and shoulder areas, and a shiner of a black eye, this is all to the left side of my head and body. I look and feel like I've just gone three rounds with the world heavy weight boxing champion!

It is hard to remember what it was like to have a completely pain-free day. I think that in the days pre-accident, that I must have on many occasions tempted fate, for whenever anyone asked me how I was feeling, my stock answer was always, 'Me? I'm as healthy as a horse.' However, I must say that I will never give up hope, and I believe that there is always light at the end of the tunnel. I was lucky enough to have been saved from under that tanker, and I'm sure that either a cure for chronic limb pain will be developed, or maybe my over active brain will one day finally get tired, and throw in the towel!

Chapter 13

ESCAPE TO REALITY

During my stay in ward twenty-eight, the bane of my life were the physiotherapists and the haematologists, the former because they always appeared to want to assess me performing some gargantuan task, and the latter for the amount of blood that they managed to coax from me, regardless of which method they had to use! I totally rebelled one day, and said that if they required any more of my blood, then they would have to let me extract some of theirs first. My threats, as usual, were totally ignored, and the needle aimed towards my groin. If you have never had blood taken from such a delicate region, then I strongly recommend that you give it a miss. It is about on par with a sample taken from the foot, yuk! I have to be honest though, there was a good reason for such unusual measures, although nothing that was directly within my control, for my poor old veins just never seemed to want to co-operate, and were in a constant state of collapse, and so other more uncommon routes had to be found. As my Mam always said, 'Enid, you never did part with anything without a struggle!' I shouldn't jest really, because the hospital supplied me with gallons of blood, before, during and after the operation, so I suppose they were only taking some of their own back. I do often wonder just whose anti-bodies are floating gracefully through my bloodstream?

It was during one of these long and arduous sessions with the physiotherapist that Eddie made a sharp exit, he slipped away whilst I was gainfully employed. He was gone for quite some time, but when he got back I found out why the need for the secrecy, it made me aware of just how special a man he was.

Prior to my run in with the tanker, I had for many years worn on my left wrist, a silver bracelet, it had been a gift from my friend Lynne. Whilst she was in Holland on holiday one summer, she had bought one for me and one for herself also. We both very rarely ever removed them and I liked to think that it symbolised the strength of our friendship. I rather sadly accepted that my bracelet had been either lost on the road, or incinerated, along with my poor old arm. Unknown to me Eddie had recalled that whilst in Harrogate hospital, the nurses had to cut away my clothing, and remove what remained of my jewellery. So on the slight off-chance that it just might have been salvaged, he went off to Harrogate to make inquiries. He managed to track it down and bring it back to me, and it has remained on my right arm ever since. He is a truly special man, and I love him all the more for his thoughtfulness. I mentioned previously that I had lost all of my clothing after the accident, well thanks to my good, old fashioned Mam I never went on a journey unprepared, always wearing my best underwear, to quote the oracle, 'Just in case you have an accident,' and so on this occasion I was wearing the most beautiful ivory coloured silk underwear, which I had recently paid a small fortune for. Needless to say the beautiful underwear went the same road to the incinerator as my arm did. Sod's law, isn't it? I still find myself following the same daft policy, even to this day, and really, what difference should it make if you are wearing your oldest knickers, so long as they save your life. I think we have another case of vanity here!!!

Nearing the end of my 'incarceration', the view from my pent house window looked very inviting, I could just about see the beautiful blue sky! The outside world beckoned, and my need for escape reached mammoth proportions, especially on days when the sun shone. So a scheme was hatched! Eddie very carefully packed me up with pillows, wrapped me in blankets and he made sure that I would not slide out of the big wheelchair, and then we made good our escape. We had to stop at regular intervals for Eddie to gently haul me back into position, as I was unable to support my back, neck and head yet. We were unbelievably adventurous, and we made our way to the staff canteen for an illicit cup of coffee, which was to be accompanied by a long and envious gaze from the rather large canteen window. Sitting there and looking out on that beautifully sunny day a strange thought suddenly struck me. I had no visual remembrance of the outside of the building. I had been rushed into it in a totally unconscious state on that fateful Friday. It evoked such a strange feeling, and I suddenly had a desperate need for my curiosity to be satisfied, so we broke all the rules, (once again!) and headed for the entrance through which I had been wheeled in such a terrible condition. We ventured sheepishly through the main doors, and though I did not recognise the surroundings, I could at least now conjure a picture in my mind's eye, where previously there had only been a frightening void. It was a rare sight indeed, a mixture of old and new buildings, and the most exciting setting that we could find, was the car park to the front of reception in Chancellor Wing. The fumes were enough to render a camel unconscious, but it felt unbelievably good to be alive and in God's fresh air. One more step to going home!

Chapter 14

OUT OF THE MOUTHS OF BABES

Matthew, our little grandson, was only four years old at the time of the accident, and he constantly asked to be allowed to visit the hospital to see his Grandma. His mother, Sara, thought that at this point in time it might be beneficial to both of us if he and his sister Faine came to the hospital for a short visit. It was more than obvious from the outcome that Matthew was finding it very difficult to understand what had happened to his Grandma. When I asked him for his usual hug and kiss, he stepped back a little, and said, 'I'll give you a kiss when you are better, Gran, I might hurt you.' It upset me to think that he might be frightened of me, but I suppose it was understandable, after all he was very young.

On his second visit he was still a very apprehensive little boy and so I tried not to worry him by forcing the situation, thankfully somewhere during the visit a little voice said, 'Grandma, have you lost your arm?' I told him that he was right, and that I had lost it, and much to everyone's amusement, a serious little voice chastised me saying, 'Then you will have to be much more careful the next time!' As the old saying goes, 'Out of the mouths of babes.' It took many long detailed chats, and many months of gentle encouragement before he achieved some real semblance of understanding of the situation, and what happened to his

Grandma. By the following Christmas he was attending the local school and I was much amused and extremely relieved when I was taken as a guest to see Matthew perform as a pirate in the school pantomime. I was taken in to see him prior to the performance, he stood up in the class, and without hesitation or instigation, he announced to everyone, 'This is my Grandma with her one arm.' I knew at last we had made a breakthrough, and he was not frightened of me any more.

During this final week of my stay in Jimmies, Eddie and I sat for many hours going over events which had suddenly and almost miraculously come back to me. I hoped that my memory and my brain were both returning to normality. My sense of humour was also vastly improved, because I began to see the funnier side of many of the things that had happened to me whilst in St James'. I remembered in my earliest stages, having the strongest suspicion that I had parted company with my left boob! Vanity again! I was exploring around under the bed covers and was shocked to find that the boob didn't appear to be where I last remembered it to be. I must have been slightly stupefied, as when I did pluck up courage to look, not only did I not lose it, but it also appeared that I had gained a third one!

This third boob resides somewhere in the region of what used to be my left armpit, the surgeon assured me that it was only the remains of a muscle, but it still looks quite unusual. My wayward armpit, now nestles brilliantly on the left side of my chest, which I might add still has to be shaved, no sweat glands but plenty of hair! Wait for it, there is more! I am even more unique than anyone could ever imagine, for during the accident, the skin from my chest and shoulder decided to take up permanent residence on the roadside tarmac, so the plastic surgeon's skill was called upon to construct a new chest for me. I now have a chest that resembles a patchwork quilt, the chest was made from what remained of the back of my left shoulder. The surgeon's skills must have been sorely taxed by the problem presented to them, but they appear to have carried out a remarkable job. I know that very few people in this world can lay claim to being truly back to front, but I can. Didn't I mention that I was unique?

I was more than ashamed to admit that after all that I had been through, I was frightened to have my stitches removed from the amputation, in fact I was petrified! What a coward I was, because it did not really hurt much at all. I stopped counting when I reached fifty, so I never knew the real total but I thought to myself, 'One more hurdle crossed.'

I believe that the faith that I had in the staff nurse who carried out the procedure, probably helped me to relax and it made for a painless removal. You see it was the same staff who had come to my aid and shown such great compassion on my first night in the ward. It took quite some time to complete the operation, and even then there must have been many stitches that healed under the skin, for on occasion, I find little pieces, wending their way to the surface even now. The wound looked very red and angry and in my eyes it was very ugly, so I did not let my eyes look on it or my mind dwell on it for long. I stuck to my previous decision to leave the great unveiling of the new me until I was in the confines of my own home.

Chapter 15

GOING HOME!

The next major objective to be tackled was going home and the first step in the procedure was to convince the physiotherapist that I could not only stand, but walk also. I would not be expected to walk far, only a couple of steps, and I wouldn't be expected to attempt it without some assistance, I did know that the deciding factor would be if I could walk aided, four steps up and four steps down the staircase. It made me sweat even to think of the task. After much practising, and loads of encouragement from Eddie, I finally made it. How I managed it I will never know to this day, for I felt that the effort would kill me, I shook violently, and the sweat poured out of me. Lying there on the bed in the aftermath of the event, trying to regain my strength and composure after the physiotherapist had left, I suddenly thought how reminiscent of childbirth it had all been, very painful, totally exhausting, but with a definite feeling of satisfaction for a job well done. I had been told that I would be in hospital for at least six more weeks and this gave me the incentive to prove them wrong. I now only had to seek the permission of the doctors on their next ward round so we both waited patiently for the team to arrive the following morning. I tried to look as healthy as I could, under the circumstances, but we were both so desperate to go home that it could not fail to have shown in our faces. I never cease to be amazed as to how great is the faith that mankind has in his home and the family environment, it is said to move mountains. It certainly moved me up and down that staircase! I know that I needed to be close to Eddie again, thinking about being in the same bed with him beside me brought me such a sense of love and security and both elements were very important in the recovery process, not only for me, but also for Eddie. I also knew that sooner or later I must take a look at what was left of me in a full length mirror, I could not put it off forever, it had to be faced.

I'm sure that the doctors must have known what I was going to say to them, for it was a subject that I had broached on one or two previous occasions, 'When can I go home?' I must appear to have been an ungrateful creature, as here I was desperately wanting to get away from the one place that had played such a major part in saving my life. In reality, I was in an emotional turmoil, for I not only desperately wanted to go home, but at the same time, I was also extremely frightened to leave the one place in which I felt so totally safe, and surrounded by the medical help that I had depended on for so long. The problem solved itself, for the doctors said that if transport was available, then I could go home, the inner panic began to abate, and I knew that I would cope.

The journey from Leeds to Teesside usually took about one hour under normal circumstances, but we realised that this journey could not be classed as normal circumstances and it would take much longer. It would need to be a very gentle, sedate drive, incorporating many stops en route. Eddie had had the presence of mind to bring his car back to Leeds with him when he had gone home to make provision for the children, and also bring back with him to the hospital his clothes and toiletries to see him through his long stay in Jimmies. He had made the trip whilst I had been in theatre, and he arrived back just in time to see me being wheeled back out, seven hours later, but still alive!

So transport wasn't a problem, comfort for the journey, on the other hand, took a little more organizing!

I still had to spend all of my time lying flat on my back, and so some method needed to be devised that would get me home, and afford me as little discomfort as was possible. One day whilst I was sleeping, Eddie came up with the solution: he took the car and went into Leeds to do some shopping, and back he came with mounds of soft pillows and cotton pillow cases. He intended to construct me a nest in the car by lowering the front passenger seat to a prone position, and then with the pillows, forming a soft bed for me to travel on. We hoped that the theory was as easy to put into practice on leaving.

On my final night in Jimmies we had lots of visitors and as usual, the ward sister was more than generous when friends, who had travelled all the way from Wales, had arrived too late. Their journey had taken them longer than they had expected, and they arrived at the end of the official visiting time. The sister very kindly let them stay for extra time, she even came and had a chat with us all, for this was her last shift for the week and she wanted to say goodbye to us both. I will never be able to speak highly enough of the nursing staff, it was my experience that they were all very dedicated people, extremely hard working, and to their patients, worth their weight in gold. If I ever get the chance to have a quiet chat to the government minister responsible for the National Health Service I will give him a piece of my mind, for I know that I am not alone in thinking that N.H.S. staff are overworked, underpaid, and are often made to feel like outcasts, if they ever have the audacity to stick up for their rights. I suspect that if the current Prime Minister were to have found himself in my position, and God forbid, he hadn't kept up his subscriptions to private medicine, I could guarantee that we would see some major changes in the system – the bulk of them being in the favour of the staff and their working environment!

One of the young doctors, Mark, also visited us on our last night, he came to say goodbye but he also had an ulterior motive, for he and Eddie had a wager about the final number of get well cards that I would receive whilst I was in hospital. He said over one hundred, and Eddie plumped for just under one hundred. Well, on the final evening, the total reached ninety-eight, and Mark said that he was going to rush out early the next morning and send me two just so that he would win. I hasten to add that the wager was purely for fun and only a verbal agreement, strictly friendly, no money was to change hands.

Anyway, as it worked out, Mark need not have worried, for by the first post next morning came another bundle of cards, they made a grand total of one hundred and six!

The room looked very sad and bare when Eddie finally packed up our belongings, and he promised me that as soon as we were home he would reinstate each and every card, and they would have pride of place until I was well again. Many months later the final and grand total came to two hundred and six, I now keep them safely filed away and when I feel that I need my spirits lifting I sit and carefully read through them, it always works wonders for my morale.

Getting dressed to go home proved to be a funny affair, for I had lost so much weight that my usual size fourteen jeans had to be held aloft with a very large leather belt. I had been ten stone twelve pounds on the morning of the accident, and I was now eight stone six pounds, fully clothed and with my boots on! I looked like I was wearing my big sister's hand me downs, or that I had somehow 'shrunk in the wash'. Still I was on my way home, and I did not care what I looked like in my oversized gear. I knew that it was an easy problem to remedy, for when I was eventually well enough I could have lots of fun running amok with the cheque book in the local shopping centre! I must have still been in a morphine induced state of euphoria, for all I thought of was that I had finally got down to a size ten, where clothes were concerned it was the beginning of a big, big problem.

When we were ready to leave, Eddie lifted me into the wheelchair and propped me up and we said a weepy and emotional goodbye to all the friends that we had made amongst the staff. Each and every one of them had proved to play such an important part in my recovery and we promised that we would come back and see them regularly. This seemed doubly important to the staff involved in the Intensive Care Unit, as so often the patients that they fight long and hard to save, lose the hold that they have on life, and as I felt that I had been one of their success stories, I thought they might like to be occasionally reminded of how important a job they really do.

The young staff nurse in whom I had such real faith waited to escort us to the car. We were both pleased to have her with us as we felt that a special bond had been formed. I must admit I felt rather apprehensive about facing the big wide world again, still I had it to face, and besides, I was a very lucky lady, for I did not have to face it alone, I had Eddie, and a loving, caring family, and the support of many friends and colleagues to help me.

The journey was made a little easier by extra shots of strong pain killer that had been prescribed for me, but even so, I felt every pebble on the road, a bit like 'The Princess and the Pea.' I dozed for a short while at the beginning of the journey, and then finally to my joy I began to see familiar landmarks, such as

Mount Grace Priory, The Cleveland Tontine and Roseberry Topping. I felt very humble to be allowed to experience these sights once again, as I had for so long thought that I would not live to see any of them. The road carried on through Yarm, and then directly on into Eaglescliffe, where I had only lived for six months. The tears would be contained no longer, for I was home and I was still alive!

When we pulled into our drive I saw Eddie's parents, Edith and Ted, his twin brother John, and John's daughter Michelle, they had travelled all the way from Birmingham just to be there to welcome us home. It will always remain one of the highlights of my life. I recalled the first time after the accident that I was allowed to talk to Edith on the telephone, I was so desperately weak, and so incredibly frightened and I knew that she was a lady with a very strong faith. I know that her faith has not faltered in over eighty years, I asked her to pray for me and I knew that she would not fail me, for Dad and her have a special quiet time, each day, morning and evening, when they will read from the Bible, and pray for family and friends, and anyone in need of help. The world would benefit greatly from a surfeit of people like Edith and Ted. God willing we shall have them in our lives for many more years to come. They prayed every day for my safe recovery whilst I was in hospital, and they have continued to do so every day since. I feel that they have been a great influence in strengthening my faith, and I hope that one day I will be able to express my faith in the way that they both can.

Mum had brought with her the makings of a delicious meal, fresh chicken and vegetables from Dad's garden in Perry Barr. I still had little or no appetite but I did manage to eat some chicken, and what's more, I managed to keep it down! The long journey, plus the exertion of the meal, put paid to the last of my strength and so Eddie carried me up to bed.

Chapter 16

MIRROR IMAGE

The next hurdle came immediately I reached the bedroom door, for in our bedroom the back wall was completely covered by a mirror fronted wardrobe, the expression 'full frontal,' took on a new meaning for me. I stared at myself, the shock must have been more than apparent to Eddie, it hurt so very much in my heart. How could I ever expect anyone not to stare at me? I was quite an unusual sight, no shoulder or arm, head almost lying on my right shoulder, a twisted spine and several inches lost from my height, and all this was with the clothes on! I wasn't at all sure I wanted to see what lay underneath the top layers. When I finally got undressed I was overcome with despair, how could I expect Eddie to ever find me physically attractive again? God forgive me, for I did him a great injustice, for the Eddie that I knew and loved, would never let the loss of my arm affect our relationship. I never fail to marvel at his love for me, to him I will always be the same person that he met all those years ago. He has given me the courage to face up to my new found circumstances.

I did not like the mirror image that stared back at me, but I knew that I had to get used to the sight, and I clung to the fact that the doctors at the hospital had said that a false shoulder might go a long way when compensating for my lack of balance,

54

and I hoped that it might make me look physically, as I had done prior to the accident. When I was tucked up in bed with the covers under my chin I felt much more in control and also much less vulnerable. To sleep in the same bed as Eddie was priceless to me, it made me feel so safe and secure, and it especially made me feel loved. Even though I was tired and weary, I kept my eyes open for as long as I could, so that I could savour the experience.

When we both finally slept it was after shedding many tears and offering many special prayers. Thank you, God, for turning a deaf ear to my selfish plea whilst I was in Intensive Care. I really did want to live!

Chapter 17

RESURRECTED MEMORIES

Lying there in our bed, day after day, I had so much time to think about my life, my family and my work, and just about every other topic imaginable. I had spent my formative years in an East Durham village known as Trimdon Station. It was then a mining village with a very close sense of community spirit. I found memories that I had long ago filed away in the deep recesses of my mind, suddenly reappeared, fresh and bright, to be remarkably resurrected. The richness of my early life could not be calculated by wealth, for it was the richness of life itself which comes from family, friends, and a way of existence that has now sadly faded into oblivion. The village has always been a stronghold for the Labour Party, and the area has known such names as Peter Lee, Mannie Shinwell, Jack Dormand, and our present M.P., Tony Blair. Unfortunately both of my parents are now dead, but I have such wonderfully vivid memories of them that they will remain alive in my heart forever. My dad was born in the adjacent village of Trimdon Grange, or as it was known in early Victorian times, Five Houses, an apt description, for that apparently was the sum total of the houses before the onslaught of the rich mine owners. My dad was called Stanley Edwin Errington, and his father was William Errington. My grandfather had not been born in the village for he was not a local man. He had in fact been born on the estate of Lumley Castle, in Chester le Street. My great grandmother had apparently been the cook at the castle for many years. In those days, if work was available, then employment would generally fall to the immediate families of the estate workers and so I do know that my grandfather did not begin his working life down the pit, the family always remember him as referring to himself as 'the castle bootboy.' The whys and wherefores of the move from Lumley Castle to Trimdon Grange pit no one seems to remember, but the likeliest explanation seems to be that he moved when he married my grandmother. Together they raised five daughters and two sons, in a strict but very Christian home. Their first home was quite big by pit village standards, but it was way before my time and nothing remains of it, so my memories are of an old stone miner's cottage, situated in an area of the village known as 'The Plantation', which consisted of rows of terraced, two up, two down, stone cottages. They were completely typical of miner's cottages within the Durham coalfield and their like can be seen at such places as Beamish Museum. Needless to say the toilet was out in the back yard, along with the tin bath, that hung from a nail on the coalhouse wall. My grandmother was christened Mary, but for some unknown reason was always known as Polly, a fact that I wasn't even aware of until after her death. She must have originated locally for I have many relatives in the area who still bear her maiden name of Welch. I only knew her as a very old lady who had survived, along with her Victorian morals, mob caps, wrap over pinnies, lisle stockings, and button over shoes, for many years after my grandfather's death. She lived until she was ninety-two, and when she died I was just seventeen. People tell me that I am like her, but if I'm honest, at the tender age of seventeen I could not see the similarity, maybe now in my mid years I possibly would. As it still is in the present climate, women seemed, then also, to outlive men, even with the rigours and dangers of innumerable childbirths in the earlier part of the century. I would sit, as a young child, listening to her explanation of how to get from A to B, which might only be a stone's throw away, but due to the intricate, and invariably long-winded explanation, it could have been a million miles. On she went, in her slightly proper voice, with its strong pitmatic accent, liberally dotted with, 'Noo onyway,' and 'The kens?'. It was a sad day when some bright spark decided that our rich and expressive pitmatic speech should be superseded by slang. Nowadays I cringe when I turn on the local T.V. station and have my ears assailed by professional actors trying to emulate an accent that they know nowt about, just because it seems to be the in thing! It also makes me very sad to think that today's generation of youth have missed the experiences of my non materialistic childhood. Not for me computers, video nasties, and drugs, and the disrespect that seems now to be bred on every street corner. I would far rather have my Mam's old clothes horse and an old sheet to make a tent in our back yard, and a candle, an old tin can, some lard and a potato, all to make chips (in a fashion!!) and have the chance to enjoy growing up as it naturally evolved, and not have it thrust at us from every angle. I was allowed to pass through my childhood without any of the premature pressures of today's adult life which seem to assail the youth of today. Polly Welch would neither have approved of or understood many of the actions of today's society, such things would have been 'beyond her ken!'

My times of really deep and nostalgic thought seemed to have almost always followed severe bouts of ill health, times when I contracted, or developed, one more, illness or setback, and during the recovery period my memories seemed to return in boatloads. In retrospect I believe that although I had many terrible injuries, the thing that concerned me most was the damage that had been caused to my central nervous system. I was so frightened that one or more areas of my brain could have been permanently damaged, so much so I made myself relive happy, and quite often very sad events. This technique seemed to open the floodgates, and helped greatly to dispel my fears. I still have many symptoms that cause me concern, one of them being the fact that after always having a remarkable nose for 'aromas', I now appear to be the only person in the car not to notice that we are driving past a pig farm, everyone else will be gagging and I am totally oblivious! Let me add that this does have its advantages!

My Grandmother Errington must have been a strong, hard working lady, for even as I remember her in her very old age, she always kept her little cottage cosy and clean, remembering that she used a sweeping brush and not a vacuum cleaner, and she still used to wash her clothes in a wash house with the aid of a copper and an old-fashioned mangle. I recall visiting her in her cottage, before the bureaucrats decided that this type of habitat should be demolished and its inhabitants moved to new council accommodation in a neighbouring village – a sad mistake for all concerned, especially the elderly. I am glad to say that it seems to have rebounded on the instigators, for now the old type of community with its eaved terraced houses and its back to back conditions, appeared to have had something going for them, as we are now seeing their like being held up as a good example, with the aim being to coax back a sense of community spirit and a pride of place that should never have been done away with in the first place! If only these 'innovators' would think before acting, or even if mistakes are made, then let them be admitted to for what they are. If I had my way, I would decree, that all of the architects and council instigators of such schemes be condemned to live in the monsters of their own creations. I would be generous, and keep the term to twenty years, then it would only 'feel' like a life sentence to them! At least I still have such marvellous memories of that little stone cottage, the centrepiece as always, being the large blackleaded fireplace with a kettle always on the hob, and the delicious smell of fresh baking wafting about the kitchen. The chenille tablecloth, the aspidistra in its big pot, the rocking chair, which was my particular favourite, the china dogs on the shelf over the fire, the tallboy in the corner, with drawers big enough to double for a cradle if there was a newborn in the house. The door was secured with what is still referred to as a 'sneck', there was no need for locks, they just weren't necessary.

The one memory that literally brings tears to my eyes is the distinct recollection of the dining-room chairs with their horse hair stuffing. You've never lived if you haven't sampled the joys and delights of being made to sit quite still, for the duration of the weekly visit, when all that separates you from the horse hair is a pair of small cotton panties. I don't think that I will ever forget just how badly it itched. It was rather a case of grin and bear it or face the wrath of my Mam, when the specific instructions were, 'Sit still, and move nothing but your eyelids!' I must have been made of stern stuff for I have not only survived the weekly ordeal of Grannie's horsehair dining chairs, but I also managed to survive the escapade with the thirty-eight tonner to boot!!

Right up until the day that she died, Grandmother, would always refer to me as 'Our Stan's bairn,' and I knew that on leaving she would always sneak me a few pennies. My Dad on the other hand, was always presented with a special favourite of his, a home made rice cake. This ritual went on for as long as I can remember, and even when her eyesight began to fail badly, and maybe the cake wasn't quite up to her usual standard, my Dad would still eat every crumb, because he knew that she loved him enough to go to the trouble of baking it just for him. She lived through many disasters, two world wars, the depression, and one of this country's worst mining accidents, the day that one hundred and twenty-six men and boys were trapped underground after an explosion, seventy-six of them perished. She told me that on that day the whole house shook dreadfully and she knew that something terrible had happened, but she also knew that she was lucky enough not to have had any of her immediate family underground on that fateful shift. There were few houses in the village that were left untouched by the disaster and the women of the village could only wait in silent vigil at the pit head until they were told who had perished. Had I known the value then of all her memories and experiences, then I would have asked more questions and listened more intently, but all children are impatient and I was no exception.

I did not have the privilege of ever knowing my Grandfather Errington, in fact, from both sides of my family, I knew only my Grandmother Errington. As fate would have it, my Mam was one of the youngest of a family of ten siblings, her mother having given birth to her quite late in life. My Mam then waited until she was thirty-eight herself before I made my entrance into the world, so consequently, I never did have the chance to benefit from a full set of Grandparents, and I did feel as a child, there were times that I was just a mite badly done to when it came to Grannies and Grandads!

These memories of family and childhood were, on occasion, completely obliterated from my thoughts, especially on the many times that I was due to have 'one more exciting enema!' or perhaps, when I had my head, face down in the toilet bowl, parting company with the ingredients of my last meal! All of which are guaranteed to make wishful memories somehow pale into insignificance!

Chapter 18

VARIATIONS ON A SHOULDER

I seemed at times to take two steps forward and then three steps back! There were times that my progress was so excruciatingly slow that I very much doubt that it could have been monitored at all. I did however have one over all aim, and that was to get back to as near normal as it was possible for me to be. When I was confined to bed for such long periods I was lucky enough to have a constant stream of visitors, there were so many that Eddie bought me a large diary to keep track of things. I carefully noted down all my medical appointments, and also who was visiting me, on which day, and at what time. I felt that I was slowly beginning to organise my life again and to do so gave me the feeling that I was still able to something worthwhile.

Gradually I became more and more accustomed to the reflection in the mirror, and I held great store in the fact that, although I could never have an arm that could be anything other than cosmetic, I rather fancied myself with a prosthesis that would look something akin to my shoulder. I was contacted by the local general hospital and given an appointment to see the doctor in charge of prosthetics. My first appointment had to be postponed, due to one of my many setbacks. When I finally managed to see the consultant, Dr Barsoum, I was once again impressed as to his dedicated and caring attitude. We had a long chat about the accident and the aftermath, and Dr Barsoum once again repeated the fact that I had been incredibly lucky to have even survived the ordeal. He was amazed as to how little time had elapsed since my release from hospital. I did not tell him how ill I really felt, but I was a lady with a mission, and I needed desperately to do what I had set out to do, in this case it was to be fitted with a new shoulder.

It was exactly eight weeks since my accident.

I was introduced to several contraptions that to all intents and purposes appeared to have been constructed in the local shipyards! I could never see myself strapped into anything that looked so cold and inanimate, they were all metal and leather, with large straps and buckles, just like a racing harness! I think that they were a little taken aback by my openness, as I kindly declined the offer of a cosmetic arm but I did accept the offer of the shoulder.

I have never regretted my original decision, but I might add that this does not stop Dr Barsoum from trying to persuade me otherwise every time that I meet him, he is determined that I should have that fake arm!

I was not well enough for quite some time after for a plaster cast to be made of my upper torso. The technician, Barry, only visited our local hospital once a week as he was based at Chapel Allerton near Leeds. He explained what needed to be done, and when the time came to take the mould he would take measurements, make a template, and also produce a plaster cast. Barry showed me a sample of the type of material to be used in the construction and I was amazed to see just how light it was, it looked very much like pink mousse. This spurred me on, and I could not wait for the day that I would be presented with my new shoulder. Looking back now, I don't know if I thought that the shoulder was going to be a cure all or not, but I did know that I needed desperately to feel that something constructive was being done to help me. I had this definite need to be normal again. Rather shamefully, I still felt then that 'normal' meant being a certain ideal shape, size, and weight, governed by the demands of the media. How wrong could I have been? I now realise that normal is exactly as we are. Whether we have one or two bits less than the next man, or one or two bits extra, we are all uniquely different individuals. This lesson took me some time to learn, but had I not realised and accepted this very important fact then I feel that I should still have been struggling to accept my personal loss.

When I finally took possession of my new shoulder, I was still too ill to be able to withstand the pressure of the straps for more than a few minutes at a time. The first official premier of 'The Shoulder Epic' came a little while after, when Eddie took me for a very short car ride to test it out for comfort. I managed about five minutes before I needed to have the thing removed, it caused unpleasant sensations of great pressure on the left lung area, and also intense pain on the amputation. So it had to be removed as soon as possible, no matter where we were. It just so happens that we found ourselves in the main car park in Middlesbrough, trying desperately to carry out the whole procedure without exposing me to the population of the town. We had thought that we were unobserved in carrying out the whole manoeuvre, but to our great surprise we spotted a lady in a very shocked state, she must have been sitting in her car eating her lunch time sandwich, and I think that we must have almost frightened her to death because she dropped the sandwich in mid bite, started up her car, and made off towards the exit at breakneck speed. I can only imagine what was going through her mind, she must have initially thought that we were having a bit of lunchtime hanky panky – or maybe the poor soul thought that I was being dismembered right there before her eyes! Anyway she did not stay around long enough to find out the truth. If she ever reads this account of what really happened, then I apologise profusely for the fright that she must have got, but I can assure her that we were only trying to remove an uncomfortable prosthesis!

At the present time, and if I'm honest, I have to admit that I do not like the fake shoulder, but I made such a damn fuss until I got the thing, that it would be less than fair of me to dismiss it offhand. The size of the thing bothered me the most, for I felt that it was larger than life, so to speak, so I had Barry reshape it for me. When we got it home it still didn't look right, so Eddie took the shoulder, along with one of his chef's knives into the garage, and rather like carving the Sunday roast, he gently pared away at it until it looked similar to the right one. Had we been seen by the children, then they might have accused us of vandalism, and I know that I would have been less than impressed if they had carried out the same practices on any of their own possessions, but needs must when the devil drives, and the end product was much more acceptable. I felt that this was justification enough, and besides we didn't get caught!!!

I have gradually made fewer attempts at wearing my 'Hunchback of Notre Dame' contraption, and when I asked Eddie for his honest opinion, he said exactly what I knew that he would: he said that he loved me, not the fake shoulder, and he felt that family, friends, and colleagues would appreciate me better as me, the unabridged version, and the people that really matter wouldn't even notice the lost bits and pieces. He was right, of course, but I feel that the path that I followed on course to the acquisition of the prosthesis is one that I know I needed to follow, and for me it was part of the healing process.

It made me look again at just what I was doing and question my own motives for wanting the thing. Or did I want to be as I thought other people would want to see me? I had to deal with it and live with the outcome. I like to think that I made the right decision for me, the shoulder now has pride of place in the wardrobe and is only given an airing for what we call in the north, hatches, matches, and dispatches, work that one out for yourselves.

Chapter 19

A DRESSY LITTLE MAN

It was autumn, and I was having one more setback in my physical healing process. I was still at the time taking copious amounts of restricted drugs as a means of pain control. Unfortunately this had a detrimental effect on my physical well being and my digestive system suffered greatly, although I think in my case it could have been termed as an 'undigestive system!' because what I didn't actually throw back, I then refused to part company with in the normal manner. I must be in possession of the world's most unco-operative bowel! My personal record stands at twelve wonderful enemas in fourteen days, I often wonder if the Guinness Book of Records can match that!!

I can laugh about it now, but I can assure you that at the time my thoughts were not much given to merriment, and it was at these difficult moments that I took my mind back once more to my past, and as always, I remembered the great fortitude with which my own Father bore his life long ill health. Sadly I lost my Dad when I was just nineteen years old, he was such a gentle man, who gave the impression that he didn't ever want to grow up, for he had a great affinity with children. He always said that he was grateful to have been born into the era that he had been, because he felt that he had seen many of the world's great achievements, historically and otherwise. He was always in awe of new technology and his interest lay in the field of medical developments and the incredible world of space flight. He did not live long enough to see the first man to step onto the moon's surface, but I like to think that he was watching it from a far greater vantage point than we were on earth. Both his skill and knowledge seemed to me unsurpassed by everyone else's Dad, to me he was an Einstein. He had many great talents, especially in things such as clockmaking and restoration of antique clocks, sculpting, metalwork, and he was a great inventor of gadgetry. He designed and built our first radiogram and several televisions, and I was the first person in my school to have an electric overblanket, made specially for me by my Dad. He had so many fine qualities that he was a hard act to follow, but luckily, I have found in my husband so many of the same qualities. My Dad was forty-two years old before I made my entrance into the world and my brothers were both quite grown up by then, Stan, who was twenty, and serving in the Royal Air Force in Egypt, and Matty who was thirteen and almost ready to enter the world of work. I can't recall my Dad ever raising a hand to me, in fact I would be hard pressed to even recall a time when he even raised his voice to me. This seems to me to be remarkable, because I must have on occasion been naughty enough to warrant a good wallop, and if I'm honest, I can remember more than one occasion!

My Dad had lost his older brother, George, to the First World War, he also was a gentle man, just like my Dad, and if the war had not intervened then my Uncle George would have taken the cloth, it apparently had been his greatest wish. Although he must have been against killing his fellow man he did his duty by enlisting in the Medical Corp to try and help save lives. He himself was killed when returning to take up his duties as a medic when the Red Cross ship that he was a passenger on was torpedoed by a German U-Boat. He was buried in France. I was given his Bible as a keepsake by my Dad and I get great comfort by always keeping it near to hand. The sisters in my Dad's family were, Beattie, Bella, Jenny, Dori and Millie, and at present, sadly, out of the seven siblings, only my Aunty Dori survives. I marvel at times as to just how much she looks like my Dad, there is such a strong resemblance, their mannerisms and characteristics are alike, their height, build and even the shape of their hands and nails are similar. Aunty Dori is now well into her eighties but she has such a wonderful memory and such spirit and strength of character, she will always be special to me. I loved my Dad, he wasn't at all like other Dads, although he was a chronic asthma sufferer since the age of twenty, and had to live his life by strict rules, nevertheless, he still had a passion for life. He had worked at the pit as a blacksmith for twenty-eight years before his health failed him. He then took a post at Wynyard Hall, working for the former Lord Londonderry, in present day terms he would probably been classed as a security man, but in those days the patrolling of stately homes was always left to the night watchman, a much more romantic figure, more so than today's equivalent. After a few more years of persistently failing health he turned his hand to barbering, a job that he pursued right up until his death in nineteen sixty-seven. In the latter part of his working life he was in charge of men's hairdressing at the local hospital for mental disorders, Winterton Hospital, Sedgefield. In its heyday the hospital must have been one of the biggest employers in the area, and many of my aunts, uncles and cousins worked there, even my Aunty Dori was a nurse there for most of her career.

The mining community in which we lived was in the parish of Deaf Hill cum Langdale and within this closeted world my Dad was always known as a 'dressy little man'. This meant that

Deaf Hill Pit as it was in author's Grandparents' time

he took great pride in his appearance and he always wore a suit with a waistcoat, the word 'little' appertains to his slight build, about five feet five inches to be exact. He was quite particular as to where he had his suits made, and his favourite tailor was a firm called 'Weaver to Wearer', I'm not sure if it is still in existence or not. I think that he was a little bit of a snob when it came to the material, for he always had to have Harris Tweed and the suits must always carry the orbed sign that Harris Tweed were famous for. On the balding head perched a matching cap which was, on the occasion of warmer weather, swapped for a felt 'cheese cutter', a term which, as a child, totally bemused me. I know now that it only pertains to the shape, and not the fact that it might be used to cut cheese with! As long as I could remember he held the belief that only genuine Harris Tweed would keep the severe northern winters at bay, for if he did not take great care he would suffer the most horrible bouts of bronchitis. Harris Tweed was his own personal antidote for germs!

In his youth, during the notorious days of the Charleston and the Black Bottom, he apparently used to cut quite a dash in his pin stripes and bowler hat, believe it or not. I still have the bowler hat to this day, it has pride of place, along with my Mam's mink stole and my Grandmother's lace blouse and beaded cape. When I'm ready then I will pass them all on to my daughter, for I know that she will treasure these keepsakes just as I do. When I think of the things that I used to play with as a child, for I used to play at dressing up in the most wonderful Victorian clothes, if only I had known their value, then I would have taken so much more care of them, but instead I played at being a leading lady in period dress.

I remember as a child, on long winter nights, sitting next to my Dad, both of us huddled in his large leather wing chair in front of a roaring coal fire. He would tell me stories from his youth, he talked in a way that kept a child fascinated, so coloured was the detail. When my Mam wasn't there, we would bake potatoes in the coal fire, barbecue steak over the glowing embers on a special wire trivet that he had constructed, and drink gallons of hot coffee, made from boiled milk, each mug had to contain at least four spoonfuls of sugar! It was just like camping out in the comfort of your own front room!

In the summer, when my Mam worked shifts in the local hospital, Dad and I would go to the seaside each Sunday, and have fish and chips, candy floss, ice cream, and a visit to the Punch and Judy show. Some Sundays we would go to the swimming baths, an art that my poor Dad struggled to help me perfect. I never did manage to master the skill, I still panic at the sight of anything deeper than my bath! Or on occasion we would have a more cultural day out and visit Bowes Museum or Castle Howard and the like. Always on the return journey we would follow the same familiar route, Dad and I had this conspiracy together, which my Mam wasn't party to, we would stop off at Dad's favourite pub. He would bring lemonade and crisps for me to the car and he would treat himself to one pint of real ale, straight from the cask. As I look back now I realise that my Mam was probably well aware of the deception but she never once mentioned it, she knew that it was our special secret.

Chapter 20

THE ART OF ONE UPMANSHIP

On one fine morning, during this time in my recuperation, I decided that it was time to make a very special journey. I had promised myself that as soon as it was possible I would do my hair, put on my make up, and dress in the way that I knew pleased my Mam. I needed for her to see me making progress, it would put her mind to rest. I decided that it was time to attempt the forty mile round trip to her house. Eddie helped me with the construction work and together we managed to make me look a little more like the successful and professional lady that my Mam liked to see. She was like lots of other mothers in the world, she enjoyed showing me off to her friends. Just the kind of thing that old ladies like doing, in fact I am convinced that the art of one upmanship was invented by the ladies of the Over Sixties Club, for they seem to carry it out so admirably, God bless them all!

The look on my Mam's face when Eddie helped me to walk into her little bungalow, was worth all the pain and effort that it took to get there. She called in all her neighbours who were all either married to retired miners or the widows of miners, for the terrace of bungalows is owned by the Durham Miners Association. I found myself surrounded by faces that I had known all of my life, members of a community who still all thankfully remember what it was like to live in the community of my not so distant childhood. It evoked such a sense of belonging to my birthplace and its people, that I suddenly remembered having the same feelings of belonging and security when I was a very little child. My Dad would carry me on his shoulders, to my Aunty Dori and Uncle Bill's house, to see in 'the first foot,' an old tradition that has long since changed beyond recognition, for it now appears to be, just one more excuse for the younger generation to get as drunk and offensive as it is possible to get, a fact that saddens me, for people seem to have forgotten the true spirit of New Year. In my childhood this spirit was more than evident, and in those early, simple days, life was unbelievably sweet for a little, blonde pigtailed girl, being carried on her Dad's shoulders to fetch in the New Year, the memory of such events will always be pure magic for me.

Chapter 21

MICHAEL

At times my spirit appeared to be as poor as my physical health, and at these times I found it very difficult to cope with the unceasing pain. It was during one of these black times that I was put in touch with a trained counsellor who had been until quite recently an ordained minister of the church. I was at the same time promised an appointment with a pain specialist, Dr Milligan, who ran the local pain clinics. I knew that if I was to make any progress at all then I needed follow every route possible for self help. The pain at times consumed me and I knew that it could become all powerful if I did not find the right combination of pain control. I also did not want to spend my life at the mercy of dangerously strong drugs, for I have always believed that these types of drugs could, over prolonged periods, cure one complaint but also be the cause of many others. I learned this from the experiences of my Dad who lived through the era when the medical profession would prescribe stronger doses, or increased amounts when the poor invalid had become used to the existing dose of drugs. I saw my Dad take dangerously large amounts of drugs right up until his death, as it was believed then that there was no alternative available.

Michael, our counsellor, entered our lives very gently, he was instantly likeable and very approachable, both Eddie and I found no difficulty in confiding in him. Our initial interview was done together, but after our first meeting we arranged to see Michael individually. Eddie was now finding that he must come to terms with his feelings, for he did not want anything that he might be unknowingly suppressing to cause us problems in the future.

We both knew that he carried such a feeling of responsibility for the accident, and the stress and trauma that such feelings can evoke can be harmful to any relationship. Eddie is himself a trained counsellor and so he knew what he must do, but like everyone else, he also needed a helping hand. This was also a testing time for me, and I had many moments of sheer panic, for never since the accident had I faced anything without Eddie by my side. We both found Michael's approach, attitude, and handling of the situation very reassuring. He appeared to have, for the want of a better expression, an 'odour of sanctity' about him, and even though he showed no outward display of his religion, he nevertheless had the air of an ordained minister.

We discussed every aspect of my personal circumstances, and I told him then that I will always be of the belief that my accident could not be attributed to any one person. It was like countless other accidents, made up of a series of small events which unfortunately culminated in forming or fulfilling all the criteria needed for a disaster. Michael taught me a form of pain control known as 'relaxation and imaging', for me this was the first step in learning to control my own particular situation. It is like a form of self hypnosis, a totally relaxed state where pain has no place, and since learning of it Eddie has helped me to take it further. I have great faith in the technique and I would urge anyone who suffers from chronic pain to make inquiries into its utilization. Eddie and I know that we can create our own special form of pain control and if I have a particularly bad day then last thing at night we use relaxation and imaging, it aids me to sleep for a while without the pain surfacing too much. It does not afford me a whole night's sleep, but it does let me rest sufficiently to restore a little of my strength and composure. It is usual to carry out the process totally independently, but I prefer to carry out the task with Eddie as my partner. In my case the factors that seem to govern the success of the relaxation and imaging procedure are as follows:

1. Total faith in the process.
2. The ability to relax the body and mind fully.
3. The belief and faith in the person who is partnering you.
4. A clear visual recall of a time and place from your past, that has been of such a significant influence on you, that you want to return there.
5. A belief in your own ability.

Michael set the practice of relaxation and imaging in progress, and we have gone from strength to strength, in fact a year after my accident we lost a very dear friend who for some time knew that his time on this earth was limited. He desperately wanted to put his house in order so as to leave some precious time for him to be with his fiancée, family and friends, he used to call this his quality time. He was so brave and so quietly determined, and he had such a love of life that he was so special to the many people that cared for him. I will never forget the last time that we saw him alive, he had such an aura of peace about him and his faith shone through his terrible pain. He asked if we would do some relaxation and imaging with him, it was a very special moment for both Eddie and me. David, our friend, managed to relax, control his pain, and he took himself back to a time some thirty years ago, to a beach in Polperro, on a holiday with his late wife and his son, who was then only young. It brought him such peace and happiness, he appeared to relive events that had for so long been locked away in his memory, and he delighted in their reappearance. God was good and he ended David's pain two days later, and I for one am happier knowing that he is at peace without pain, on a beach in Polperro, in the sunshine with his beloved wife. God bless you David, and thank you Michael.

Eventually both Eddie and I began to lay the ghosts of our accident, and Michael felt that we had a very positive attitude to our future life together, so, as gently as he came into our lives, he said goodbye, and went off to help others.

Chapter 22

THE HAND THAT ROCKS THE CRADLE

As time passed, my Mam seemed to get over the shock of my accident a little and began to regain a little of her enthusiasm for her beloved game of bingo! She had a passion for the game for more years than I care to remember, something that I never really understood, probably because I could never see any attraction in the pastime. Though her spirit appeared willing, the flesh was not well enough to manage the long bus journeys to and from the nearest bingo hall, so to while away the long evenings, she got into the nightly routine of making supper for herself and her next door neighbour, Mrs Hill, or Bella as my Mam liked to call her. They would play cards for pennies, and reminisce, all the way back over the past eighty years, to their childhood. They had both been born in Deaf Hill and had remained all of their lives there, so, as you can imagine, what they didn't know about the village and its inhabitants, just wasn't worth knowing!

My Mam had been born Sarah Jane Henderson and lived all of her young life in a part of the village known as 'The Foundry', the name having survived far longer than its owner, for although my Mam was sure that such a building did exist originally, she could not recall it being in existence during her lifetime. As in many pit villages, the small areas or individual estates within

80

Coffee Pot Street

Commercial Street, Trimdon Colliery

them, all had their own rather unique titles. Names such as, The Colliery, Byrefields, The Hilly Howly, The Dumps, and the best one for me will always be, Coffee Pot. My Mam always told the tale that its name originated from one of the many small shops in the main street of the area. The shop belonged to a pot mender, for in those days people in the village couldn't afford to throw away a pot with a hole in, it had to be patched and mended. The shop sign that hung outside the premises was an enormous coffee pot, and so ever since, and to this very day, it remains as 'Coffee Pot'. I often wonder if any of today's generation ever stop to think and question why it has such an unusual name? I only hope that in some dusty archive somewhere, someone has the facts recorded for posterity, for it would be a shame to see part of our mining heritage totally forgotten.

My Mam's family lived in Church Street, and as you have probably guessed, it ran parallel to St Pauls Church. My grandfather worked all of his working life at the local pit, as did most of the male population in the village. My Mam was the third youngest of ten children, that is the ten that survived, goodness knows how many pregnancies my grandmother actually went through, as in most families in those early days, it was not uncommon for mothers to lose half of their offspring in either childbirth or to some childhood ailment such as diphtheria, scarlet fever, whooping cough and T.B. and many more things. Thanks to the marvels of modern medicine these no longer exist to cause any major threat to our society. My grandmother was Sarah Henderson and my grandfather was Matthew Henderson, family names that have been repeated through the years, my daughter is Sara, and her eldest son is Matthew. The Henderson children were, George, Matthew, Mildred, William, James, Annie, Mary, Sarah Jane, Thomas and

Isabell. These 'Sunday names' were shortened for everyday use to George, Matt or Matty, Millie, Billy, Jimmy, Annie, Mary, Jenny or Ginny, Tommy and Bella. There is only one sibling left, and that is my Aunty Bella, who is in her eighties now. My Uncle George died in the trenches in World War One, whilst he was serving with the Seaforth Highlanders, and I have in my possession an old sepia photograph of my Aunty Millie when she was very young, dressed up in his uniform, standing next to my grandmother's dining room chairs. I still have the same chair, it is one of a pair, and I guard it with much family pride.

My Mam told me that although my grandfather was head of the house, it was my grandmother who reigned supreme, or as I have often heard my Mam say, 'The hand that rocks the cradle, rules the roost!' As a child, I had so many visual reminders of the late Victorian and early Edwardian eras that it was easy for me to conjure up vivid pictures of my Mam's childhood surroundings, and I would have loved to have savoured the closeness of existence in the earlier part of the century in our village. It seemed that my Mam and her peers could amuse themselves with all manner of pastimes, all of which would be classified as unfashionable nowadays, but let me tell you that when she started to relate to me the things that they got up to, I used to roll about laughing.

One story she told me was of the days long before disposable nappies were even thought of, when the mothers of small boys were in the process of toilet training their offspring; as the story goes, the mothers would leave the 'offending appendages' dangling from the front opening of the babies' trousers, this was supposed to allow for any slight mishap that they might have whilst playing outside, it meant that the child could pee without soiling the clothes! Remembering that this was a poor community where spare clothes often did not exist, it may sound funny to us nowadays, but it was apparently a common thing to see such sights in the earlier part of the century. Anyway, this unusual habit was the bane of my Mam's young life, she was horrified that one day, someone would lose their apparatus to one of the ducks and geese that roamed quite freely through the gardens, looking and scratting for worms! She never did tell me if her worst nightmare ever came to fruition, and I have to admit that although I've never been an advocate of disposable nappies, they would have saved my poor Mam a lot of worry if they had been invented in King Edward's day!!

Another story related was how, as a young girl, my Mam almost got into very serious trouble. Even in those days she always seemed to be in the forefront if anything untoward or mischievous was about to be carried out. This fact seemed to have followed her through life, for she was never one to back down from anything that she had started, caution was a word that rarely existed in my Mam's vocabulary, in she went, feet first, every time! This particular night, when the evenings were beginning to 'draw in', a term we use when the winter evenings are fast approaching, my Mam and her gang of friends decided to play a trick on a neighbour. The lady in question was what we call in the north, 'rather stout', or to the layman, quite fat. She was also of the opinion that she was just a little bit above her neighbours and she was known as 'posh, or a would be, if she could be!', but no matter how grand she thought she was, she still on occasion had to avail herself of the loo. The loo was situated outside, generally across the back yard or down the garden, and they were always known as 'netties' or 'middens'. They apparently got the name netties from the common practice for the loo to be surrounded by chicken wire, something like a perimeter fence, the wire resembled net, hence the terminology. These netties had no running water to flush, no lighting, and definitely no drains, the ominous task of emptying them fell to the 'midden men'. There was a door to the front for access and a small trap door to the rear for the midden men to clear out the debris.

The occupants of the house used to tip the spent ashes from the fire onto the said debris to make it a little easier to remove. Anyway, a plot was hatched, and as usual my Mam drew the short straw and was delegated to lead the assault. She positioned herself behind the trap door in the dark, feather duster in hand, and waited for the fat lady to perform her nightly ablutions. The rest can be imagined, for out came the lady, up went the skirts and petticoats, down came the bloomers, and as you can guess, my Mam scored a perfect bullseye! The fat lady screamed and screamed, not realising that it was a childish prank, and believing that she had been molested by a pervert. The hue and cry that followed was quite a serious matter, everyone turned out to apprehend the criminal, the men searched the streets, and the women comforted the fat lady, who was by then suffering apoplexy! Fortunately for my Mam, she was never found out, the criminal was never apprehended, and eventually the search was called off. No one ever got blamed for the 'dastardly deed', and I know that the ewwxercise was never repeated by my Mam, but whether or not it taught her a lesson in life, I'm not too sure, because she remained a very determined lady, right up until the day she died, and I heard her say that the fat lady lost one or two airs and graces after the incident! I on the other hand, was always too timid to follow in her footsteps, this determined characteristic, seems to have missed my genes but it certainly has not missed my own daughter, for she can be just as determined as her Grannie ever was!

Chapter 23

PRECIOUS POSSESSIONS

During my childhood I never lacked for the important things in life, especially not for love and affection, as these two elements were always very much in evidence to me. Although I wasn't born until two years after the end of World War Two, rationing was still in force and many of the creature comforts were not easily available, but I was lucky to have hard working parents who never let the lack of commodities affect my young life. Having said that, I feel that I must follow up the statement with the fact that neither was I a spoilt child. I was taught to look after my possessions as they could not be replaced if I misused them in any way. I remember when I was just three years old, getting up on Christmas morning to find that Santa Claus had brought me a new doll. She was at the time a new concept in baby dolls, for she walked and talked in fact she uttered the word 'Mama' when tilted forward, nevertheless she was futuristic to my young eyes. She was a Pedigree doll, and I took such good care of her that each subsequent Christmas she would be revamped, she would be provided with a new wig, of differing length and colour, and a whole new ensemble would be knitted for her. She remained in my possession until quite recently, when in 1990 my Mam took it upon herself to pronounce my doll as being 'past her sell-by date!' and she despatched her into the rubbish skip, without my consent I might add! She couldn't see why I was so furious, and I can tell you that we had more than one or two words over the issue. I couldn't seem to make her understand that she had thrown away part of my childhood memories, all my Mam saw was an old broken doll. I never could comprehend how a lady who never threw anything away in her life could be so blasé about my poor old doll.

Each Christmas, along with my revamped doll, I would get one new item, a doll's pram, a cot, a little wooden bed, a doll's house, all came my way, and all of which I cared for with much love, in fact I coveted them so much that I would not let anyone else touch them, just in case they got soiled or broken, I must have been a selfish brat! I still have most of them to this day; Archie Andrews, a ventriloquist dummy from the early fifties, he nestles in the bottom drawer in my bedroom, almost still in mint condition; Muffin the Mule, a string puppet lies beside him, he was made famous with the onset of the television and by the efforts of a lady called Annette Mills, and a soap model of Mr Turnip, still all in one piece, miraculously, having been lovingly cared for over the past forty years. All toys and names from the not so distant past, that have long since been superseded by Sindy dolls, Stars Wars, Gladiators and computer games. I often wonder just how many of today's children will relish their toys enough to look after them for a lifetime? If my own children are anything to go by then we won't see many Antiques Roadshows in the future.

In my Mam's childhood toys were a very rare commodity, they came at the back of the list, far behind things such as, rent, food, clothing and medicine, which always took priority. If there was any spare money it would be put by for a rainy day, and when presents were afforded with large families such as my grandmother's, then gifts often had to be shared with another sister or brother. So when it was my Mam's turn to get a new doll for Christmas then she was expected to share it with my Aunty Mary, because of Mary's gentle nature my Mam used to boss her around, even though she was two years Mary's junior, and my Mam could be much more devious than my Aunty Mary would have ever dreamed of being. All things apart, they did however have a rare closeness, and especially after they were both widowed, remained constant in maintaining the family ties. The time that I spent in my Aunty Mary's home will always remain special to me, it was always crisply clean, and echoed with much love and laughter. As I said before, it was expected that Jenny and Mary should share their beautiful Edwardian doll. Even then my Mam was a force to be reckoned with, and she decided that she wanted the doll all to herself, but for once she did not get her own way as my Aunty Mary had the very same idea! Well, they managed to fight for most of Christmas Day, and finally my Grandmother made them put the doll aside. She ruled that they both learn to share it or they would have to do without it. It took some time to reconcile but they knew that they were beaten, so they decided to share the doll. To their dismay they found that they had left the doll on the front room settee, and they arrived just in time to see one of their older brothers accidentally sit on it. The doll's head, being made from porcelain, did not survive the ordeal, and it broke into many pieces. Again my Mam learned a bitter lesson from life and after that she always remained one of life's givers, she never was a taker. She said that she believed that God decided that both Mary and herself needed a short, sharp lesson for being so selfish, and that's just what they got! Maybe God was doing the same to me when he decreed that my Mam should throw my doll into that skip, he gave me a delayed lesson in sharing!

Chapter 24

AN END TO THE IRONING!

Still thinking along the lines of selflessness, I remembered just how unselfish Eddie was, and still is. He gave me every minute of his time, it didn't matter if it was night or day, if I needed assistance he was there, smiling and helpful. He never once complained when visitors seemed to arrive by the boatload, he cheerfully fed and watered them, even though at times I knew that he must be feeling more than a little jaded. He always managed to keep up both of our spirits and did everything with a smile, but I was sensible enough to know that the strain could not be kept in check indefinitely, he needed a rest from all the work and responsibility. I worried about him doing too much, and carrying all the burden of the housework, cooking, shopping, all of this coupled with caring for me was far too excessive for just one person to cope with. I began to get very frustrated because I was helpless in taking some of the burden from him, in the past we had always shared the jobs entailed in running the house, and now it grieved me that I was not able to be a partner to him in such things. My greatest worry was the fact that it was almost time for Eddie to return to his job as a college lecturer, for he was nearing the end of the summer vacations, and I knew that arrangements must be made if he was to return to work with a clear mind, and also he needed to be sure that I was being cared for whilst he wasn't there. Help came our way via the local authority, in the guise of a ministering angel named Doreen, she was and still is a registered care assistant, a very apt title in Doreen's case, for that's just what she is, very caring and a good friend. The marvellous thing was that Eddie could return to work knowing that I was safe in her more than capable care.

She helped me bathe, dress, and prepare for the day ahead. We also found the answer to every mother's nightmare, namely, the mounds of ironing that had been created by what appear to be several hundred teenagers, (even when you know that there are only three residing in the house!) and who all seem to spend their waking hours creating a cleaner environment by transferring all of the world's dirt onto their own personal apparel. As you can imagine it took very little persuasion to get me to avail myself of a washing and ironing service run by a local lady. Ironing was one of the housewifely jobs that didn't rate very highly with me, even when I had two hands with which to perform the task, I did it because it was necessary, not because I enjoyed it! Now it is impossible for me to do it. There aren't many perks for someone in my position, but getting out of doing the weekly ironing must be number one! My Mam felt very badly that she was unable to help me with my work, but she was suffering from the affects of old age that had been so aggravated by many years of very hard work. She had spent her lifetime looking after her family and she had on occasion had to keep more than one job on the go, she had always been able to put most people to shame when it came to hard graft and enterprise. I recall that when I was a small child of about two years of age my Mother ran a fish and chip shop, she also helped my Dad with his smallholding, ran the home, and also took in a lodger. My Dad, although a semi invalid most of his adult life, was at this time employed at Wynyard Hall. The land that the smallholding was on was very close to our home and my first clear memories of it were filled with pigs, hens, turkeys, geese, baby chicks and a little pony called Jimmy, he belonged to my brother Matty. My doll's pram on more than one occasion provided a home for the runt of the sow's litter, and as young as I was, my Mother told me that I had a modicum of success and managed to rear one or two piglets that to all intents and purposes would have died if left to the attentions of the sow. They make very unforgiving mothers and generally kill the runt of the litter. The sad thing was, that once I had reared them, I had to then watch them being carted off to the mart when their time came. Luckily I was blissfully unaware of their fate!

At the Christmas of the same year I was standing by our kitchen window, watching my Mam despatch several of our chickens, no doubt for family and friends to enjoy on Christmas Day, and, not knowing what was really taking place, decided to take a closer look at the proceedings. I opened the back door to receive the biggest shock of my young life, for I was bowled, base over apex onto my behind by a headless chicken, which was running for all its worth past our kitchen door. I wasn't to know that the chicken had already 'met its maker' and that the reflex action of its muscles was the only thing keeping it mobile. I thought that the devil himself was after me, and it took a lot of persuasion on the part of my Mam to convince me that we did not have a headless horseman loose in our back yard!! Let me add that it did not stop me enjoying the poor old chicken on Christmas Day, in fact to my young and innocent mind, the two things did not appear to be in any way related.

Unfortunately at this time my eldest brother, Stan, did not play a big part in my life, for he was twenty years my senior, and during most of my growing up years was serving in the R.A.F. I have always regretted that we never did get to know each other as we should have, for when he finally left the forces to settle back in the village I was about to marry and leave the village for the following nine years. I always had the feeling that our relationship was more like uncle and niece, rather than brother and sister. Sadly he died at the age of fifty-four, and it saddens me to think that I never got to know him as I would have liked to. Matty on the other hand, was always around in my formative years and therefore was always 'my big brother'.

It must have embarrassed him to death, to have me trailing around after him, I can't imagine it did anything for his street cred! He did on occasion get his own back though, and when he was forced to babysit for me, he would tease me by buying chocolate and then eating most of it himself, and then feeding the remainder to the dog, leaving me crying. I remind him at every opportunity of his wicked ways, when I must have been the blight of his life. I understand how he felt though, for he was sixteen, and I was three, so I forgive him his misdemeanours!

He is past sixty now, and has grandchildren of his own, and when Christmas comes round each year I never fail to hear him relate to them just how strongly he believes in Santa Claus. He tells the story how when he was very young, way before I was born, how he had begun to doubt in the existence of Santa Claus, and so one Christmas, when he was getting a little too big for his boots, he announced to the world that he was now too old to believe any more. He was riding high for a fall, and fall he did, for when he rushed down stairs on Christmas morning, fully expecting to find lots of gifts from you know who, he did find his Christmas stocking hanging up, but it contained no toys, just cold ashes from the grate. He never imagined that his declaration of the day before would result in no presents at all! You can imagine the effect that it had on him when my Mam reminded him of his indiscretions, for Santa must have somehow overheard him. Well he started to cry, and vowed that for as long as he lived he would never doubt in the existence of Santa Claus, amid all the tears a knock came to the kitchen door and guess who was standing there? Right first time! Good old Santa! And he had brought my very repentant brother a special delivery, a tiny black pony, my brother immediately named him 'little Jimmy', because he was so small. We had Jimmy for many years, in fact I mentioned him earlier for he resided on our smallholding. Matty still carries the memory of that painful experience and wild horses wouldn't make him utter anything other than that he still truly believes in the existence of Santa Claus. Each year when the festive season looms we are reminded of the tale by my brother, and how Santa Claus taught him a lesson that he would never forget! I often wonder just who was inside that red suit? It couldn't have been my Dad as he was in the room at the time along with my Mam, and my eldest brother was then in training for the R.A.F. I still like to believe that it was the genuine article, and I'm a good girl, for I never tempt fate by doubting in the existence of 'you know who!'

Chapter 25

BUILDING EMPIRES

My Mam was, for her time, a great empire builder, and like many people from the same era she believed that there was much to be said for 'putting your money in bricks.' When I was seven years old she hatched a new business scheme which, for a time, ventured her away from frying fish and chips. One day she placed in my hand a small red notebook and a childsize pencil. The instructions were to walk to the top end of our street where the pit offices were and look for the large poster in the window of Dr Russell's old house. The doctor was long since deceased but his widow still lived there. I was told to very carefully transfer all of the details from the poster into the little red notebook and then return home to her immediately. I was totally unaware as to what was going on in her mind, but in those days I did as I was asked to, to not have done so would probably have resulted in a smack on the leg, and I wasn't a very brave seven year old. Besides, the general rule of thumb was, messages that were carried our properly always brought some form of reward, and as I was as keen as the next man when it came to cream biscuits or a slice of jam and bread, I carried out the task to the best of my ability.

Looking back on it now, I realise just how daring this new venture of my Mam's was. Up until this point in time we had lived in several houses in my short years but this one was something quite special. My Mam's plan was to buy the large house from the doctor's widow, Mrs Russell. She planned to convert the front section into a general dealer's shop, and the rear would become our living accommodation. I think that this time she even frightened herself with her boldness, and I was never quite sure if she had even informed my Dad as to her intentions!

Once my Mam had made up her very determined mind then she could not be swayed. We moved into the big house in nineteen fifty-four, and believe it or not, it still remains in my possession to this very day, my daughter, her husband, and her children still live there. I did not at the time realise the enormity of the amount that my parents had paid for the property, even though, on the first of each month, I was despatched on the bus to West Hartlepool, to the building society office in Surtees Street. The instructions were to hand in the sealed envelope containing the exact amount which had been carefully put aside to deal with the payment. I did not realise for many years just what it was that I was doing, but I did know that it was important enough for me not to lose the envelope. After my Mam's death I inherited a small, very old, brown leather handbag which had obviously seen better days, but its condition belied the importance of its contents, for this little bag was very special, it contained her precious memories, memories that are now just as precious to me also. In the bag were our old wartime ration books, school certificates and school reports, my brother Matty's Boys Brigade papers, a letter to my Father from the late Lord Londonderry, and tucked right down in the bottom corner was the little red notebook that I had used all those years ago. Next to it lay the paying in book that I had so dutifully taken to the Building Society Office every month. When I looked inside it turned out that my parents had paid the princely sum of nine hundred pounds for the property. The going rate at the time for a two bedroomed terrace house was about one hundred pounds, and a completely new semi, with bathroom and inside loo was in the region of four to five hundred pounds, so you can see why this was quite a big venture, especially for a lady who left school at the age of fourteen and whose only expectations had been of a domestic nature, for in those days, a woman's place still very definitely was in the kitchen.

So we moved up in the world to live in Nostell House, Station Lane, Deaf Hill. The house had been called after the famous Nostell Priory, unfortunately it was a name that I never seemed at ease with, and I was always very reluctant to give my address as anything other than, 81, Station Lane, Deaf Hill. I had somehow got it into my young head that the word Nostell was in some way related to the word nostril!

In my childhood lots of words were thought of as 'not being nice', so nostril in my eyes was on par with words such as belly

Deaf Hill early in the 20th century. Nostell House is at the end of the street on the right hand side.

button, armpit and bottom!! I was not going to chance uttering such words, just in case it incurred parental wrath. I was never quite sure what might happen if I was ever tempted to swear or blaspheme in any way. Maybe I would be instantly transported to the devil, and being a devout coward, I preferred not to tempt fate! Silly when you think of it, but it really did give me cause for concern. I was therefore more than relieved when my Dad found out about the 'nostril syndrome' and explained to me the error of my ways, and that all the time I had been making mountains out of molehills! Nowadays I find the modern day society an entirely different kettle of fish, my naive ways seem almost unbelievable when compared to my present day counterparts. I often wonder if this 'new' society was ever created in the name of progress, but I think not, for when I hear infants and children using language that would make a squaddie cringe and I see teenagers rampaging about the streets, stealing cars and looting other people's property, their actions recorded for posterity by C.C.T.V., I doubt very much if any social progress was ever on the cards to begin with! I feel sad that I appear to be turning into a middle aged cynic, but I find it very hard to come to terms with the regression which is now so apparent in mankind, I feel that it is such a waste and a sure route to extinction. I am glad to have grown up when I did, and although I had lots of time during my convalescence to deliberate over the problem, it will take someone far more knowledgable than me to even attempt to find a solution.

Chapter 26

THE BABIES CLASS

I still had my long term plans for my future firmly set in my mind, but my powers of recuperation had other plans. I found that my immune system seemed to have almost been wiped out, so I went from being a very strong healthy woman before the accident, to an invalid whose system was being attacked from all sides by every germ and virus known to man. I fell foul of everything going and again spent long spells when I was too ill to get out of bed.

Once again I escaped into my past and my early school days. I always found it a great advantage that we lived so close to the school, I only had to walk a few hundred yards and I was into the school yard. I was lucky enough to be able to leave the house at five to nine and still make the assembly bell at nine, some of my friends had to battle through autumn fogs and winter snows, for it took them at least fifteen minutes to walk from the other end of the village where the council estate was situated.

I started my school life at Deaf Hill School at the tender age of four, my Mam had also attended the same school for her own education, many years previously. Miss Carter was my first teacher, Miss Carters's 'babies' class was a very pleasant and gentle introduction to the education system, and the only real worry that I and my friends had at this young age seemed to be

The Babies Class

Deaf Hill School
Circa 1913 – In Author's Mother's time

Deaf Hill School
Circa 1998

who could take home the dirtiest plasticine board on a Friday afternoon, and who could bring back the cleanest board on Monday morning! All very serious stuff for a four year old. Miss Carter was a good teacher and a nice lady, she obviously enjoyed her work and she devoted her life to introducing the village children to the joys of learning. I imagine that in those days each village school had a resident Miss Carter, an unmarried lady who had dedicated her life to her work. My Mam would have been a little less than kind regarding her marital state, and would have referred to her as 'a good bit of stuff gone to waste!', typical of pit village humour.

I began my education in a class of mixed sexes, but at the tender age of seven segregation reared its ugly head and the small boys in our class were made to transfer to an all boys school in another part of the village. I had just started to get used to the small boys in our class when they suddenly disappeared. If the onslaught of the secondary modern system had not been thrust upon us then I would have most certainly completed my school days in the atmosphere of an all girls school, blissfully unaware of the opposite sex. Instead, at the tender age of eleven, having failed the second half of the Eleven Plus Examination, I was sent forth to venture into the world to attend a new secondary school, one mile away in Trimdon Village. Puberty and the opposite sex seemed to come into my life at breakneck speed. Puberty was something that I had awaited eagerly for a long time, its onset meaning that I was in the process of growing up and becoming a woman, and even though I say it myself, I appeared to cope with it admirably, whereas I was much less impressed with the opposite sex! I found that I wasn't much taken with the majority of eleven year old boys, they all appeared to be quite spotty, and at times they were just down right grotty!!! Their main aims in life at that age seemed to be either standing under the open school staircase, looking up the girls' regulation uniform skirts, or desperately sneaking a look into the girls P.E. changing rooms in the hopes that they might see a glimmer of exposed flesh. What they expected to achieve by such behaviour, was beyond my very naive comprehension, for thinking back, the greater majority of girls in our class had not even began to develop, their chest regions still being remarkably flat and boyish. Let me add very quickly, that this situation changed dramatically in the ensuing years, for as the flat-chested girls visibly changed into young women with breasts, then so did the aims and objectives of the male half of our class!!

I'm glad to say that life in Miss Carter's class was a much simpler affair, I do not even think that it had crossed my mind that boys and girls were sexually different, the things that I noticed were that girls wore skirts and boys wore trousers, girls played with dolls and prams, whilst boys played football, cowboys and indians and took great pride in making the girls cry for some unknown reason. It was a very uncomplicated life, I paddled along blissfully unaware of what lay ahead in the regions of sexual awareness. Thankfully this realisation was many years hence.

Even the seasons appeared different in those early school days, I vividly recall that we had four marvellous and uniquely distinct seasons: autumn meant golden days, thundery weather, and right in the middle of the season we had holidays for potato picking week; winter was really winter, white and crisp and most years we had mounds of snow which blocked the roads and on occasion closed the school. These times were devoted to snowball fights, igloo building, and of course, sledging, every child had a sledge that had been fashioned in the pit's blacksmith shop. Spring followed along with its fresh greenness, and it was

Miss Carter – in her 'Babies Class' (5 year olds)

Deaf Hill School in Author's time

a wonderful season for a small child, I used to like to think that the trees were dressing themselves in their new green suits, all in readiness for the beautiful summer season which was soon to follow. The summers of my childhood were long, hot and unforgettable, it must have rained on occasion but I can't seem to recall even one bad day or even black clouds for that matter, it seemed idyllic to me and my friends. We were allowed lessons in the school yard, country dancing, nature walks, sports days in the school grounds, trips to places of historic and educational value, such as castles and museums, and we even had the occasional extended playtimes – what more could a young child want? Well perhaps I can think of just one more treat that was wonderful on a hot day, and this treat was provided by my Mam.

It was during these long hot summer playtimes that she would slip me an ice lollipop through the wrought iron railings of the school yard. My Mam was never a one for convention and she put her own interpretation on certain school rules, especially when she thought that the rules in question were just a little too harsh for small children. So the lollipop through the railings technique was invented. We managed to run the gauntlet for several summer days, until one day I was caught by Miss Carter, clutching the offending lollipop in my hand just as the school bell was rung. She immediately thought that I had disobeyed the rules and had left the school grounds to pay a visit to the shop. Before I could try and explain someone snitched on my Mam. Sadly there weren't any more lollipops after that, but the pleasure of those forbidden sins, perpetrated on such long, hot summer days, will never ever be replaced in my memory.

This is a photograph of the author in 1953 wearing Victorian clothes, ready for the fancy dress competition in the local Gala held at Trimdon Station Recreation Ground.
This photo was taken at the time of the Lollipop Through The Railings incident.

Chapter 27

AN EYE FOR A BARGAIN!!

My Father was a man before his time, for he must have been the greatest living advocate for the cause of recycling that ever was. My Mam used to pull his leg about his overwhelming urge to pick up any discarded, bent or rusty nail that he came across in the road, nothing was regarded as anything other than 'a great find', which was always needed for some new venture. I think that his policies on recycling were borne out of a lifetime having to mend and make do, and it was also tempered by the fact that although both of my parents were very hard working, they were by no means able to afford everything that they needed. My Father's workshop was at the rear of the house, in days gone by it would have been termed as the 'back kitchen' where in general the cooking and laundry was done. It was an Aladdin's cave to my young eyes, full of unusual treasures, a bit like a more recent Steptoe's Yard! We had hundreds of jam jars, each full of nails and screws of every size, shape and denomination that was conceivable to man, motoring magazines dating back to when 'Adam was a lad!', copies of the *Beano* from as far back as 1948, and a large work bench. The bench was used for a variety of pursuits such as welding, soldering, sawing, sculpting, wireless and T.V. repairs, watch and clock making, and the cobbling of shoes. It was also home to the gold fish bowl and underneath it the dog used to sleep! The list would be endless if I really put my mind to thinking about it. So it is little wonder that I am following in my Father's footsteps when it comes to collecting curios, my particular love is Art Deco ceramics. Although I must add that as a child, my taste in just what I collected was not quite as discerning, for in my formative years I must have been this country's youngest jumble sale junkie!

My eyes used to light up when I came across a poster advertising a forthcoming jumble sale, any local venue would suffice, Church Hall, Welfare Hall, Methodist Chapel Hall, Salvation Army Hut, or even the local school, to name but a few. I could indulge myself buying second hand babies clothes with which to adorn both my doll and our poor long suffering dog, who used to look like some old Victorian teddy bear, when he was swathed in matinée jackets and bonnets, and forced to take pride of place in my dolls' pram. Needless to say he enjoyed every moment of the dressing up, for he was always bribed with endless packets of digestive biscuits!

I must confess that I had another motive for going to jumble sales, and that was the fact that in general, the ladies of the different fund raising organisations would always present for sale to the public such delicacies as toffee apples, home made cakes and pies. I could leave the pies and cakes alone, but heaven help me, I never was able to resist a toffee apple, not even to this very day!

So as soon as the doors were proclaimed open on the day of the jumble sale, then I would rush in and buy my threepenny toffee apple, and wander off to see what bargains I could unearth. I recall one such sale taking place at our little school, after buying my goodies I managed to find some beautiful Victorian baby clothes. I proudly took them home to show to my Mam. I went into our kitchen via the back door and carefully

106

dressed up my doll, when I was satisfied that she looked her best, I then paraded her and myself in front of my Mam and her shop full of customers, hoping for approval. Everyone gasped in sheer amazement, but to my surprise I was very quickly ushered out of the shop and back into our kitchen.

I could not understand the hurry, but once in there, my Mam told me that my beautiful lace baby dress was not to be displayed in public again, for the people in our village were very superstitious, and I had in my innocence purchased for my doll a Victorian shroud, the type that they 'laid out' a baby in prior to burial! It was not one of my more successful purchases, I might add!!!

I was not to be deterred, the next jumble sale was soon to follow and it was to be held in the local Church Hall. Off I went once again, with my pocket money clasped tightly in my hand and this time I made the most wonderful find, just as I entered the hall I saw a pair of amazingly small, ladies' high-heeled shoes. I could not believe my eyes, for I was all of seven years old, and to my way of thinking, just the right age to start wearing high heels! Once again I parted with my threepenny bit and I became the proud owner of a pair of tan coloured, size two, ladies heeled brogues. I thought that I was the 'bees knees'. I decided to wear them to walk home and make yet another entrance and surprise everyone with my eye for a bargain. While wending my way to the toffee apples I suddenly had an idea, with my remaining threepenny bit I would try to find a gift for my Mam. Martyrdom took over and I forwent my toffee apple, and looked about for a suitable gift. I could not believe my good luck, for there by the door was the most wonderful statue of a beautiful lady in long flowing skirts. I was besotted by my find, and so eagerly handed over the last of my pocket money.

I marched out into the sunshine, clip clopping along in my

new high heels, taking particular care not to trip up, or worse still, drop the beautiful lady, who I might add, was all of eighteen inches high. I carefully turned my lady around to face the world, for I just knew that everyone would want to admire her. I was right, for both the statue and I caused quite a stir. Everyone that I passed smiled and spoke to me, and almost everyone said what a lovely statue it was. Even strangers pointed, the local bus driver waved at me. I was as proud as punch! I even got a wave from the old men on the bench outside of the local Miners Welfare Hall. After a long precarious march home, I finally sat my lady on the kitchen table and it felt very good to have been the centre of attention, what with my new shoes and the statue, my Mam was going to be really pleased with me this time! Just then my big brother, Matty, came into the room, and as usual his mind was on other things, for he was engaged, and soon to be married. Give him his due, he did listen to my story of how everyone had admired my statue, and how we had caused quite a stir in the front street. With this he decided to turn and take a look for himself. When he caught sight of my purchase to my great dismay he roared with laughter. I could not believe it, why was he in such hysterics? His raucous laughter fetched my Mam from the shop. She came into the kitchen and I proudly presented her with the beautiful lady. She took one look and she started to laugh, she laughed, and I cried, I cried in dismay, for I thought that she did not like her present, but I was wrong, for she wiped my eyes, told Matty to keep quiet, and thanked me for the beautiful gift, and she said that she had just the right spot for it in her bedroom. I must have had a very sheltered upbringing, a simple and naive existence, for she gently explained to me that my beautiful lady was totally devoid of clothes from the navel upwards, a fact that I hadn't even noticed!

Now that I look back, I smile to myself as I recall all of the

108

smiles and stares that I mistook for admiration. In my innocence I only saw a very beautiful lady, it never occurred to me that she was bare breasted, for naked was a word that did not exist in my childish vocabulary. Sadly that day I may have entered the 'big' world, by learning one or two grown-up words, but even more sadly I lost the innocent naivety of a little seven year old in high heels!

Chapter 28

A LIFETIME OF CORSETS

As I very slowly made progress with my struggle against pain and ill health, I eventually came to a stage where I found it necessary once again to return to wearing outdoor clothes. Up until then I had managed by improvising with the clothes that I had worn previously, but if I'm honest I'd have to admit to looking like a sack tied in the middle, as everything 'fit where it touched' so to speak. There was also one essential difference, I had several bits missing, and those bits were necessary to achieve a balanced look where fashion was concerned. As I began to achieve a little more mobility, I hit upon a major problem with my apparel, what on earth was I going to do without a bra? Before the accident I had always had to wear a bra, as I was what people classed as 'well developed', and even after losing so much weight, I still found that I couldn't go out into the world 'unfettered'.

We made lots of enquiries at many different lingerie suppliers and found there was a distinct lack of underwear for ladies with only one shoulder, I appear to be the sole member of a very exclusive club and 'we are not catered for!' So once again we had to call on Eddie's ingenuity to solve the problem, and because he had to utilize a bra that had been manufactured to be supported by two shoulders, he had to devise a method to

110

support the left shoulder strap. He found that the simplest method worked the best, he used ribbon to slot through the loops at the back of the bra and then tied them very firmly into a bow. This lifts my left boob to somewhere it anatomically should be! The most upsetting thing for me is that I will never be able to ever again dress myself, I will always require assistance. It is still one of the things that I find difficult to cope with as it makes it very evident to me that I will never again be independent.

It is quite ironic, for when I sit and consider the whole thing I recall as a small child that one of life's great trepidations for me was that each morning it was my job to help dress my Mam. Not an easy task let me tell you for my Mam was very Edwardian in her choice of undergarments, in fact her corsets with their whalebone stays were the bane of my life. Not only did I have the ominous task of forcing her into her pink, lace up stays, as she called them, but it also fell to me to have to purchase the offending garments from the local ladies shop, twice yearly. This was an awesome responsibility for such a little girl. Each time I left the store, carrying the corsets wrapped up in brown paper and tied with string, I prayed that the string would be strong enough to withstand the arduous journey, through the streets of our village and back to our house. I'm still not quite sure just what I would have done if all those whalebones had made a last ditch attempt at freedom, I would probably have disowned all knowledge of them and left them to fend for themselves on the pavement!! My job as my Mam's dresser continued for many years and I learned to cope quite well with one or two of her idiosyncrasies. She always had an extremely sensitive skin, and could never bear to have any pressure or friction on her shoulders, so she devised a method where I had to place under her bra straps on the shoulder area, a pad of soft linen. She also had a great abhorrence of ever getting stray hairs trapped against her skin, and I became an expert at rooting out any offending stray fallen follicles. These dressing rituals had to be carried out each morning before I went to school. I never cease to be amazed at myself, for after all those years of searching out stray hairs, why ever it was that I chose to take up hairdressing as a profession, was beyond me at all! As my Mam would have said, 'Enid, there's nowt as queer as folk!'

The situation with the corsets continued on for many years but fate seemed to take a hand in their demise. In the late nineteen fifties everyone in the world seemed to be 'going modern', and much to the chagrin of my poor, long suffering Dad, so did we. Out went the heavy carved furniture and it was replaced by the most awful looking melamine rubbish, which to all intents and purposes looked, and felt, as if it had been manufactured from old orangeboxes. To make matters worse it was all beige, a colour that in my eyes should never have been invented, it was a 'nowt nor summit of a colour!' Whoever introduced the colour beige to the world must have thoroughly disliked his fellow man. My Mam, on the other hand, thought that it was unbelievably fantastic, and God bless her, she loved every horrible inch of it. We found ourselves the proud owners of a cocktail cabinet, complete with glasses, shakers, and cocktail sticks, a dining table which extended to seat six people, with matching padded P.V.C. chairs. She did redeem herself a little in my Dad's eyes, for at the same time, having also disposed of his favourite armchair, she bought a new red leather three piece suite, and my Dad fell heir to a rather large, wing back chair, which was forever after referred to as 'my Dad's chair' – even after his death we still thought of it as his. I was not at all impressed with the modern look, I yearned for the old, battered, familiar furniture, I knew every crack and crevice of the old stuff, this new furniture was taboo, not allowed to touch, not allowed to sit on feet, just in case it got punctured, not allowed to sit the dog on it, what was life coming to if me and my old dog couldn't snuggle up together on the settee by a roaring fire on cold winter's nights? We did all manage to show the new furniture enough respect to convince my Mam that we liked it too, but guess who committed the ultimate sin of causing the new furniture considerable distress? My Mam's corsets, that's who! They ran amok one day when she sat down rather heavily onto one of her lovely padded dining room chairs, the stays could just not cope with the strain and one of them did actually make a break for freedom, it burst through the clothing and then on through the padded seat and on into the wooden frame of the chair. If my Dad had not rushed out and fetched his pliers, then she might have been there still! He rather generously extracted her and her corsets from the chair, and he never said a word. I suppose he thought that it was embarrassment enough, and besides the chair was beyond repair, and would never be quite the same again, especially now that it had a gaping hole in rather a prominent place. It was banished to a secluded corner of the room, where hopefully no one would ever notice the offending rip, we adopted the policy of 'Least said, soonest mended'.

The outcome of the whole event was better than I could have expected, for we saw the very sudden introduction of the Playtex Boneless Corset! Not only a new concept for my Mam, but a great relief for me, no longer would I fear the escape of those dreaded monstrosities, the new corsets were very amiable and never once did they attempt to embarrass me by leaping from their box in broad daylight. Oh the joys of modern corsetry, or maybe it was divine intervention?

Chapter 29

MATCHES AND DESPATCHES

That autumn was being very generous to us, and we had many bright sunny days. I always felt better when the sun shone, in fact I still feel that the sun's warmth helps to relax the tense muscles in my reconstructed neck, which in turn eases the physical pain slightly. Although it offered some ease, the sun's warmth could not take away the feeling that I still had a very long way to go in my battle against ill health and the frightening nerve pain that seemed to me at times to be unmercifully relentless. I think that if I am blatantly honest, even at this early stage I had realised that the pain would never go away. So I decided to plan my life around the worst scenario and if I had to learn to live with chronic pain then I needed to explore every avenue for myself. The one thing that I did not want to do was to become dependent on dangerously strong drugs, this I felt was the road to self destruction, both physically and mentally. I decided that at the appropriate time I would wean myself away from them. As I said previously, I remember my Dad taking handfuls of very strong drugs, and I shudder to think of the side effects that he must have suffered, not least of all the fact that they weakened his heart and this eventually killed him. He used to say to me, 'Asthma will be the cause of my death, but that's not what they will record on my death certificate.' He was right, for the cause of his death was recorded as coronary thrombosis. History rather cruelly repeated itself, and my eldest brother, Stan, died from the same condition. Some time has passed since I made the decision, and I have managed to reduce my intake of drugs almost completely. I only allow myself to take them when the pain becomes so unbearable that I can't control the muscle spasms.

On one of those bright sunny autumn mornings, Eddie took me on a very special journey, we had always planned to marry and now that I was a little stronger, we decided to make our wedding the next major objective. That day I was in need of having my spirits lifted and that's just what Eddie did, for he took me on a visit to York which had long been a favourite of mine, only this time it was to be an extra special visit, for it was on this day that Eddie bought my wedding ring.

The Minster stood tall and strong in the sunshine, I never will cease to be in awe of the magnificence of such structures as York Minster, and I like nothing better than to sit in some quiet corner and conjure up images of all the people who must have walked the well trodden aisles. I find it incredible to think that it has survived so many centuries, and still has the ability to appeal to so many different races and religions. We went to the undercroft, where we sat and held hands, we did not need to exchange many words as the strength of our feelings must have been more than evident to any spectators, and so after we had said what we needed to say, Eddie placed the plain gold band on the third finger of my right hand. The only time that I have been parted from it was on our official wedding day, which took place on October twenty-fourth of the same year.

After making the decision as to the day and date that we wanted to get married, we checked with the registrar, and found that the only time available on that day was nine ten in the morning, and so fate decreed that we have an early start to our married life. We knew that we had to be realistic about the whole event as there were many things to take into consideration, the most important being that I was not well enough to do the preparations or the carrying out of all the responsibilities and organising entailed with a big wedding. We also knew that we had such a multitude of family and friends that we were in the position of either inviting everyone or just keeping it to our immediate children. We made the decision to throw open the civil ceremony to anyone who wanted to spectate and keep the official reception to just the four children and their respective partners, and, of course, last but not least, the grandchildren. Finances also had to be taken into consideration, for at the time we were only just keeping our heads above water, so along with the open invitation to all and sundry, we extended the promise of drinks and a slice of wedding cake.

We went ahead and ordered the cake, flowers and wine, and then kitted everyone out with new clothes. When all the groundwork and preliminaries were done we heaved a sigh of relief and sat back to catch our breath and await the big day. At the time we could only see blue skies ahead, then a very large black cloud, suddenly heralded one of the saddest days in my life, for on the fifth of October, my Mam, who was so looking forward to the wedding, died unexpectedly from a massive heart attack. The pain of her death and the void created by the fact that she just wasn't there any more, defies description. Her death had been the furthest thing from my mind. Ironically the black suit that Eddie had bought for me to wear at out wedding was worn to attend her funeral. My Mam had not seen it when it was purchased so I made sure that I wore it and looked as she would have expected me to look at her funeral. I remember with good humour, just how contrary she could be if she thought that the situation required her to be! As I've said before, my Mam could never have been described as anything other than of being in possession of a 'very determined nature.' If she ever disapproved of how I was dressed, then it was never left unsaid! One day, when I was on my way to a very important meeting, I called in beforehand, to see how she was, as it was part of my daily routine to see if she needed any shopping or medication. I felt that I looked very smart and did not expect the response that I got. She was sitting in her favourite armchair, by a blazing fire, she always kept the temperature in her little bungalow at nothing less than tropical. Smiling, she opened with the statement, 'You're not going out dressed like that, are you?' this was closely followed by, 'Those trousers are far too short!'

Right I thought, I've got you this time. 'This isn't trousers Mother, this is a skirt!' Not to be thwarted, she came back with, 'Well, the skirt is far too long!' I think I got the message, regardless of what I had said, she just did not like the outfit. So as you can imagine, God forbid that I did not do her proud at her funeral!

Although my brother Matty and I were both devastated by her death, we knew that we had to carry out her last wishes to the letter, for she had very decided views when it came to funerals, and especially about her own, now we had to see them through. We had been informed on many occasions as to her wishes for the whole proceedings, but we always dreaded the day that we would have to put it into practice.

My Mam had always wanted what she termed as 'a good send off', something that was embedded in pit village tradition, and I like to think that we did her proud. She had planned for the occasion for many years, and when my Dad died in nineteen sixty-seven, she even went so far as to purchase the plot next to his in the graveyard, she truly believed that they would be one day united again in the next world.

Sarah Jane wanted to look her best and I had instructions, to see to the jewellery, and also to the hair, for she wanted to be looking her very best when she met my Dad again. She also left strict instructions concerning the transportation to and from the church and cemetery, for both family and friends.

Every single person that required it was to be seated, and all in order of seniority. To accommodate everyone in the family, we had to hire the entire fleet of mourning coaches, all that the funeral director could supply! She also requested that a bus be hired to take friends and neighbours to and from the funeral, this was not done for effect, but done out of concern and consideration, for she knew that so many people who would want to come to pay their last respects would more than likely be elderly. We had to cater for all mourners and so we hired a local firm to cater to supply a buffet, and friends very kindly offered to serve it at my brother's house, for my Mam's little bungalow would have been too small to accommodate everyone. In my Mam' old fashioned eyes it was all part of the etiquette that everyone should be well fed. There was to be sherry for the ladies and spirits for the men. She had to be 'laid away properly', her instructions carried out to the letter, this would be the last thing that we would ever do for her, and so we had to do it right.

When the day came to say goodbye to her the sun shone brightly and it remained a beautiful day throughout. She never did like the cold and the rain. Not long before she died, my brother's son, Matty Jr. had taken up the post as the cemetery attendant, and my Mam had been the instigator of a standing joke with him, she maintained that, when he finally planted her in the ground, then he had better make it a warm dry spot or she would come back and deal with him later! Not a threat to be

118

taken lightly, for even if she was there in spirit only, she still would have made a formidable opponent!! I could not have survived the day without Eddie's help and support, I needed to muster all of my physical and emotional strength to be able to carry it off, and afterwards it took me many days to recover, but I would have done it twenty times over if I knew that it had pleased her.

Chapter 30

FINAL GOODBYES

There isn't a day that passes that I do not think of my Mam in one way or another, but always the memories are pleasant ones. I even hear myself quoting her and using the same common sense logic that she used on so many occasions throughout her life. Her humour is always evident to me, and never again will I be able to pass any man in a flat cap, without smiling and remembering her stories.

When my Mam was young, the 'silver screen' was in its infancy, and she told me stories of going to see the magic lantern show, at the local Temperance Hall, which was situated closely to her home in Church Street. She also went to the local picture house to see the latest silent movies, she grew up with such names as, Mary Pickford, Douglas Fairbanks Snr., Charlie Chaplin, Pearl White, Buster Keeton and so many, many more who are now considered to be classics. The local picture house was in another part of the village, known as Byrefield, I remember my Mam pointing out a tumbledown old building to me as a child, and saying that it used to be where she watched the silent movies, I thought that it was so derelict that it could never have housed anything more important than a few head of cattle, but she would be right. It was apparently owned and run by a French couple, my Mam always referred to them as Madame Marki and her husband, you have to understand that I have spelled the name as she pronounced it, the correct spelling is lost in the past. As in all good stories, Madame Marki was a big, dominant woman, who appeared to 'rule the roost!' and her poor husband used to be small and insignificant, and somewhat under the thumb. One thing that I find quite amusing is the fact that the couple employed a pianist to accompany the silents, and strange as it might sound, the lady was blind, my Mam always called her 'blind Sarah'. Her job was made possible by her companion who would prompt her to change the music as the plot thickened, or changed in any way. I can only imagine that good pianists were in short supply, as it could not have been easy to hold down such an unusual job without the ability to see the screen. My Mam always maintained that in the early part of the century, things like blindness and crippling disorders were commonplace, and so it was in no way thought of as strange. My Mam would freely admit that she did not always have the money to pay for her ticket into the picture house, so she would attach herself to some unsuspecting male, totally unromantically, I might add, that was the furthest thing from her mind! She always had the good sense to take along as her chaperone, my Aunty Mary, who usually had to buy her own ticket because she was employed. She made completely sure that these unsuspecting males met the required criteria, the first thing was that they could afford the ticket, and the second and possibly the most important, was that they must be in possession of a bigger than normal sized head. You are probably at this stage, as bemused as I was before she enlightened me to the fact that the local shop sold a portion of monkey nuts for the princely sum of one half penny, and the general rule of thumb was that the recipient's cap was used as the measure for the nuts! Get the picture yet? Big head, large cap, therefore more nuts for your money, which of course my

Mam would share in. She was incorrigible. So now you can see why I find it quite humorous to see a man in a big flat cap! I like to think that my Mam showed great business acumen, even at such a young age.

On the day that Eddie and I were married I took with me a locket containing photographs of both my parents, I was determined that they would not miss the event. It certainly turned out to be a day to remember, we never imagined that so many people would turn up to see us married. The chapel in the registry office usually seated forty-five, it must never have seen the like before, as standing room only was the order of the day. So many of our family and friends came to help make it a very special occasion for us both. Afterwards, when Eddie and I cut the cake, and I listened with pride to my husband's speech, I'm sure that in my heart I heard a voice that I knew so well saying, 'May you live as long as you want, and never want as long as you live.' It was my Mam's favourite toast, and she never failed to use it to toast the bride and groom at all our close family weddings. She hasn't left me, but lives on in my heart and memory as a truly remarkable lady. From my wedding bouquet I took one red rose, to dry and use as a keepsake, and I had my daughter place the bouquet on my Mam and Dad's grave.

I find it very hard to visit her final resting place, I find it even harder not to think of that little bungalow as still being her home, and the worst hurt is that I will never see her again in this life. My daughter Sara felt the loss of her Grandma very deeply, and was only able to come to terms with the loss when, one night after the funeral, she had what she terms as 'an out of body experience.' She awoke in the night to find herself, not in her own bed, but standing in the children's bedroom, at the foot of Matthew's bed. She said that she knew instinctively that it was snowing outside, even though she knew that it was still only mid October, she looked out of the window and into the street and she saw an unusually bright light coming from the vicinity of my Mam's bungalow. She felt that the light was drawing her towards it, she was at first very uneasy, but she suddenly recognised her Grannie in the distance, and immediately felt completely at ease with the situation. She can never relate the following events without she gets very emotional, but she holds great store by the fact that she spoke to her Grannie, she touched her, and kissed her face, and smelled the familiar smell of her favourite perfume, and she swears that she could even feel the warmth of the fabric of my Mam's favourite camel hair coat. She tells me that her Grannie was tall and erect, just as she had been many years before, that she suffered no pain, and that her greatest desire was to go on to the next world to be with my Dad, but she could not go until she had made sure that Sara was alright, and that she had come to terms with her death. My Mam then said to her, 'My time has come, Sara, and I have looked after you since you were a little girl, but you have to let me go now, I have got to go to be with your Grandad.' They kissed and held each other for the last time and finally said their last goodbyes, and then my Mam walked off into the same beautiful light that she had appeared from. Sara awoke the next morning and phoned me straight away to tell me her story, and also that because of what had happened to her, how she now felt that she could now accept her Grannie's death a little better, for she now felt that my Mam would have wanted her to come to terms with it. She was overjoyed that her Grannie was now free from the terrible pain that she had suffered in the latter years of her life. Whether or not you think that my daughter had an out of body experience, will be governed by your own personal beliefs, but both Sara and I truly believe that my Mam had a hand in the whole proceedings, for she always maintained that, if there was any way possible, after her death, to let us know that she was alright, then she would do it. Sceptics will say that Sara imagined the whole thing as a means to helping herself come to terms with her own grief, but the one thing that I omitted to mention until now, could be the deciding factor for you also, as it was for both Sara and me. See what you make of the following strange facts: Matthew, my grandson, was at the time about four years old, and he awoke on the morning after his Mother's unusual experience, and rushing straight to Sara, said, 'What were you doing in my room in the dark, Mam, and why was it snowing outside my window?' Questions that neither she nor I could possibly answer, but maybe they are best left unanswered.

Chapter 31

TIME TO FACE THE WORLD

As you can imagine, up until this point in time, I had spent my recuperation enclosed in a loving protected world, surrounded by family and close friends. My contact with the outside world was very limited and generally I dealt with things from the great vantage point of my own home, so it came as quite a shock to come face to face, with the cruel unforgiving, hostile big wide world. I had sat for so many years on the side of the fence where it was 'safe', and I was classed as 'normal'. I had, God forgive me, been as complacent as the next man in my attitude to the needs and feelings of the less able members of this world. I was blatantly guilty of being 'normal' and never giving a second thought to what it must be like to be deprived of one or more of one's physical abilities. I was brought down to earth with a more than sudden bump, for I was not prepared for the reaction of the everyday man in the street to my changed appearance and so very obvious disability.

I find it relatively easy to cope with the curiosity of the very young, in fact their innocent questioning can be quite refreshing. I never mind being tapped on the leg by a two year old, and asked, 'What did you do to your arm?' The incredulous look on their little faces when they realise that the arm isn't just tucked neatly up inside my jumper, and that the sleeve is really empty, is something to behold. They even on occasion think that I am playing a childlike trick on them and have been known to feel inside the sleeve to catch me out. This generally embarrasses the parents but it never fails to amuse me. I even had one eight year old grab my left boob, and announce to the world that he had found where I was hiding my arm! It caused me great amusement, but his uncle was absolutely mortified, and went a bright shade of red!

I can honestly say that the younger generation cause me very little distress where my disability is concerned, it is their adult counterparts that do the lasting damage. The immediate reaction from the more mature element of the populace can prove to be devastating and demoralising to the morale and confidence. The assumption that they automatically make is that the physical disability must be accompanied by a mental disability. On the whole I am treated as if I am deaf, dumb and blind. Why is it that the older we get, the more we seem to think that it is out God given right to be hurtful and rude? They openly stare, point, nudge their companions, and pass comment in a very loud voice. I can remember my Mam doing similar things, thinking that all the time she was just being sympathetic. Maybe it can be attributed to the time, and environment that she grew up in, as in those early days almost all disorders were then classed as mental disorders and the poor recipients were all lumped together and incarcerated in the local workhouse, even the poor unmarried mothers were dealt with in the same vein. So, although my Mam's and her generation's attitude was not forgivable, it was somewhat understandable.

It is hard to believe, but I have had supposedly mature people circumnavigate me several times, halting me in my tracks, this has happened in the street and in the shops, their natural curiosity far surpassing the level of rudeness that is expected from people in their age bracket. I find that they stare at me as if I am an exhibit, and then to make matters worse, they add insult to injury, and just walk away as if I never existed in the first place.

I have run the gamut of all kinds of emotions, from pain and hurt, right through the spectrum to sheer anger, where I retaliate by giving the offenders a good tongue lashing. This way of dealing with the problem is never the real answer, for it is not within my nature to be venomous enough to deal with it, and therefore, I feel that all I do is to reduce myself to their level, and that's not where I wish to be.

I have found that, on occasion, I can throw the more sensitive members of the general public, by being very tolerant of their rude stares, and enquiring of them, 'Should I know you, I felt that I must, because you were staring at me?' It tends to leave them a little lost for an answer, and I hope, somewhat embarrassed. As of yet, I do not have the answer to every situation that life throws at me, in fact, I find that my reactions can vary from day to day, even when given the same set of circumstances. So many raw emotions come into play, that I do not think that anyone could have a set criteria for dealing with such situations, and such situations are not predictable enough to be dealt with logically. I enjoy life too much to let little things like rudeness and ignorance make me lock myself away, so hear this, you members of the general public, you will have to learn to deal with problems like me, for medical science is such that I will soon be joined by many more people, who in the past would not have been lucky enough to have survived the injuries that they had sustained in accidents such as mine. Think again, and pray that you are never forced into similar circumstances, before you even try to understand such disabilities.

Chapter 32

SPECIAL PEOPLE

'What makes us what we are?' and 'Why is it that one person appears to be able to cope with life, and the next man can't?' 'Where do I get my strength from to get through the really vicious days of pain?' These are all questions that I have repeatedly asked myself. I like to think that God gives me the strength, he also gave me a good grounding with my experience of life, by the way that I was brought up, the loving community that I lived in, my hard working and loving parents, my supportive family, and my greatest asset, Eddie. I feel that I have always been a very lucky lady, and possibly I inherited my Dad's mild manner, patient ways and his quietly determined attitude. Or maybe I am like my very determined Mam, whose hard working and 'never say die' fortitude was so much in evidence? I hope that I am a blend of both. Anyway, whatever the formula is, it appears to have gotten me through to this point in time, and although the prognosis for my future isn't what I would have liked, I am at a point where my life now seems to be on a more even keel. I must admit that it has not been an easy ride for me, far from it, but my advice to anyone faced with a similar problem as mine, would be simple: Don't ever give up the fight, hang on to life ferociously, it's more than worth it. Take charge of your own life, and have a say in your own method of pain control.

Never lose the ability to laugh at life, for it is necessary for survival. Do only what you feel good about, for there is great personal satisfaction to be gained from a job well done. Never be too frightened or proud to ask for help, it doesn't make you any less of a person than the next man. Make the most of close relationships, and enjoy every minute of quality time that you are allotted. Never ask of life, 'Why me?' for it is soul destroying, and creates a bitterness that can be far reaching, and it can affect the lives of those closest to you. Remember that you are as good as the next man and probably far braver than most, for it takes a very special kind of person to win through when thrown into such disabling situations. Finally, keep your faith, and thank God for your life.